American Thought

IN THE TWENTIETH CENTURY

Crowell Source Readers in American History

DAVID BRODY, *General Editor*

The purpose of this series is to provide students of American history
with a means for approaching key problems through the evaluation of
the historical evidence. Each of the volumes in the series concentrates
on several major issues relating to one area of American history. The
editors have chosen documents that focus on those issues in an
immediate way and from a variety of contemporary standpoints.
Each section contains a solid body of evidence for the study of the
topic being covered. Introductory essays that set the issues in their
historical context are included in each volume and each section is
preceded by a headnote that relates each document to the theme of
the section. The objective of this series will be fulfilled if the student
is enabled to think independently about the issues contained in these
volumes. The titles in the series are *American Foreign Relations in the
Twentieth Century*, edited by Manfred Jonas; *American Thought in
the Twentieth Century*, edited by David Van Tassel; *The American
South in the Twentieth Century*, edited by Robert L. Brandfon; *Industrial
America in the Twentieth Century*, edited by David Brody; and,
forthcoming, *Urban America in the Twentieth Century*, edited by
Milton Spiezman, and *American Politics in the Twentieth Century*,
edited by John Braeman.

American Thought

IN THE TWENTIETH CENTURY

Documents Selected and Edited by

DAVID VAN TASSEL

University of Texas

Thomas Y. Crowell Company / *New York* / *Established 1834*

For ETTA MAY AND WALTER R. VAN TASSEL

Preface

ALTHOUGH the selections in this book are necessarily restricted to a few areas of American intellectual life in the twentieth century, they are, however, sufficiently representative and long enough to reflect the thought and convey the mood of a large segment of the intellectual community. In addition to keeping textual excisions to a minimum, I have retained the authors' original footnotes, not because they make delightful reading, but because I think it important that the student of intellectual history see the sources of influence and information from which the author consciously drew. For example, the two Supreme Court decisions included are not only significant landmarks in constitutional interpretation but important examples of sociological jurisprudence, which could not be fully appreciated without knowing the nature of the sources upon which the majority opinions are based.

My sources for this book are acknowledged at the beginning of each selection, but my debts go beyond citations. I am grateful to my graduate assistants, Jack Cargill and especially Marilee Clore, who ably handled correspondence as well as searching out obscure books and periodicals for material. My wife Helen shared in many tasks and every day grows more indispensable as critic, typist, and proofreader. I should like to thank David Brody, the editor of the series of which this volume is a part, for his fruitful idea, his patience, and editorial reticence. The errors of omission ought to be more numerous than those of commission, but in any case the responsibility is mine.

D.V.T.

Contents

Introduction

IN JULY, 1900, *Munsey's Magazine* noted an event of passing interest—the first automobile race in America. The race took place on the Merrick Road on Long Island, April 14, with five gasoline and three steam vehicles and one electric carriage taking part, over a fifty-mile course. The winning vehicle, the electric carriage, covered the course in two hours, three and one-half minutes—an average speed of about twenty-five miles an hour. *Munsey's* saw no portents for the future in the event, other than the possibility that "before long automobile races are likely to become as common as bicycle races in this country." The automobile, nevertheless, quickly became the focal point and symbol of all the developments —and problems—of an urban and industrial age. The increase in the number of automobiles, from 8,000 in 1900 to 1,258,000 in 1913, put heavy demands on city, county, state, and federal governments for paved streets and highways.

The country's population of 72 million in 1900 was increasing rapidly through immigration. Four hundred thousand immigrants arrived on America's shores in 1900, and in 1907 the flow of immigrants reached a million a year. Cities from New York to Chicago to San Francisco were growing at an explosive rate, with all the consequences of rapid growth—especially slums. Americans suddenly became acutely aware of the evils of the new urban industrial society into which they were rushing. The problems of unemployment, poverty, slums, corruption, sanitation, disease, industrial accidents—all came in for attention by journalistic muckrakers and social reformers.

These social, economic, and political problems, coming in the wake of the transition from an agrarian-rural to an industrial-urban society, first evoked a sympathetic and humanitarian response among Americans aroused by the suffering of individuals. Eager to do something immediately, people like Jane Addams, Florence Kelley, and Lillian Wald launched the settlement house movement in the 1880's, while Jacob Riis cried out against slum tenements in *How the Other Half Lives,* John Spargo pulled America's heartstrings with *The Bitter Cry of Children,* and Nathan Straus opened pasteurized milk stations to save the lives of babies. In 1904, Sarah P. Decker shattered the composure of the assembled members of the Federation of Women's Clubs when she flatly declared: "Ladies . . . Dante is dead. He has been dead for several centuries, and . . . it is time that we dropped the study of his inferno and turned attention to our own." In the same year Robert Hunter published his book *Poverty,* a summons to concerted social action. Hunter argued, "If poverty were due purely to individual causes, it would perhaps be fair to deny the moral necessity of national inquiries at periodical intervals into the condition of all the people and especially of the poor. But no one knowing the many active social causes of individual poverty and misery could deny this necessity in a democracy of professedly Christian people." But not until 1907, in *Sin and Society,* did sociologist Edward A. Ross define the problem that would trouble intellectuals. He set forth in this book the philosophy of the new reform movement and described the way in which forces released by industrialism had transformed the old questions of good and evil, which he called "new varieties of sin." Ross called attention to the underlying problem of reevaluating moral responsibility in a period when self-reliant individualism was rapidly disappearing. Sin had incorporated. Sin was collective or social and therefore a responsibility of the whole society in an organized capacity, that is, of government.

The skein of interdependencies characteristic of an industrial society makes the sources of evil difficult to locate, and individuals themselves enmeshed in the "system" feel hidden, anonymous, and to that degree less responsible. This is only one of many characteristics of the strange new era of industrialism that Americans would have to discover, cope with, or adjust to in the first half of the twentieth century. Great changes have come about in culture, indeed in the surface of the earth, since that first motor car race on Long Island, but none is so great as the revolution in our knowledge and view of the world.

In 1950, Frederick Lewis Allen attempted to assess and explain the differences between 1900 and 1950 in *The Great Change*. Most of the changes he discovered were tangible ones of technology, fashions, manners, morals, and movies—symptoms of a much deeper change in ideas. The revolution in ideas and attitudes has altered the tone and texture of our culture. This revolution affected less perceptibly, but no less radically, the character of Americans.

The changes in ideas and attitudes of Americans are inextricably part of the country's history. Ideas are transcendent, immortal, and international, but they are conceived, understood, and used by individuals who operate within national communities. Hence, the idea of democracy, although not limited to any one nation or time, nevertheless has had a particular history, which gives it a unique meaning in the United States, inexplicable within the context of any other nation or time. One of the characteristics of democracy in America is the emphasis upon the ideal of individual freedom and the sanctity of human life. Indeed, one of the major concerns of American thought has been the nature and scope, guarantees and responsibilities of individual liberty. The concept of the freedom of the individual has undergone constant change as Americans wrestled with the problem in light of new knowledge and conditions. This is a major theme of the selections in this volume, namely, the effort to enlarge and to secure the freedom of the individual in the new urban industrial society of the twentieth century.

A primary issue of the first decades of the twentieth century revolved around the role of government in our democratic society. Quite obviously an ever-increasing number of Americans were suffering oppression stemming from industrialization that was rapidly eroding economic independence, individual opportunity, and individual freedom. The storm of debate that raged during the eighties and nineties over the necessity for reform, although not over by any means, had shifted to the question of means. A few Americans argued that the whole capitalistic system was at fault. Most agreed that an unrestrained capitalism had resulted in a plutocracy that had corrupted politics and undermined democracy. Reformers of all persuasions eventually came to a solution that in some way or other involved government action. The question was just how far the government should go. Was the government merely responsible for regulation, or was it to be made responsible for creating desirable conditions for social welfare? The obstacles to altering the federal government's traditional role were popular awe of the Constitution and the Supreme Court's severely limited view of the scope of the powers of the federal government in social and economic fields under the Constitution. Many thought it was necessary only to return political power to the people and awaken the middle-class citizen-voter, informed by the facts, who would then pass the remedial and regulatory legislation. The rest would be taken care of by the uninhibited flow of progress toward a new republic in which a great new culture of industry, technology, and science would flourish among free individuals.

By 1920, however, a second major issue of the new century was coming to the forefront of public attention—the question of the freedom of the creative individual in the business and technological society. While disillusioned progressives mourned the fate of the country in the hands of a business elite, artists, poets, critics, and novelists defended a different aspect of freedom. They pointed with horror at an efficiency engineering and technology that turned men into automatons. The biggest threat, however, was not technology but the materialistic values of a business society. Businessmen had been the most successful in utilizing science, particularly technology, while basing their claim to power on the popular Horatio Alger values and virtues of late-nineteenth-century Victorian America. The creative leaders of the 1920's aimed to shake the basis for these values and explore new horizons of individual freedom. These explorations resulted in cultural discoveries embodied in the new art, poetry, and drama, as well as new manners and morals.

Business society fell of its own weight in the great crash of 1929, bringing to a head still another major issue stirring the great depression of the 1930's, that of relativism. The relativism of the thirties not only attacked authorities and absolutes in all fields, from religion and morals to art and science, but also attacked man's very ability to discover objective truth or even his capacity for objectivity. The proponents of relativism sought freedom from the authority and determinism of an older science, aesthetics, ethics, and law. In freeing men from all absolute standards of conduct, the proponents of relativism did not envision a chaotic world of conflicting guidelines, but were impelled by a faith in the essential moral goodness of men and the belief that history would prove their direction to be the right one.

The decades of the Second World War and the Cold War saw the re-emergence of an age-old issue—how to preserve individual freedom in an immoral world. History had not proven the world to be made up of men of good intentions, as the relativist reformers of the thirties had assumed. Yet there was no hiding the fact that science and philosophy had undermined the faith in the existence of absolutes. Are there then human rights? Whereon do you base the rights of life, liberty, and the pursuit of happiness? And how do you secure individual liberties against the tyranny of the majority? Is there, indeed, a moral law, a universal yardstick by which to measure the difference between good and evil, truth and error? If there is such a universal ideal, or if we cannot survive without fundamental law, where is it to be found? How, and by whom? The paradox of the decades since 1945 is that man at last has at his fingertips the ways and means to control his environment, to destroy civilization, to create life, to control minds, yet he appears to be less in control of his destiny than ever before in history. He is unable to solve the most complex problem, always present, but now more than ever at issue—the problem of human relations and of controlling human behavior in the use of limitless power.

PART I

The Quest for Social Freedom

(1900-1919)

A̲T THE OPENING of the twentieth century, an aroused humanitarian concern for human welfare joined with scientific and technological developments that seemed to furnish the tools to alleviate suffering and thus enlarge the dimensions of freedom. Natural science had broken out of the static confines of the mechanistic view of the universe characterized by Newtonian physics. The pragmatism of William James and the instrumentalism of John Dewey (Selection 1) brought a new activism to the realm of social ideas. The new philosophy urged bold experiments as the only means of adaptation in a plastic universe in which change is the essence of reality.

The industrial revolution had already transformed American civilization, and by 1914 the United States would lead the world in production of manufactured goods. Industrialism had also brought about an urban revolution, as Americans moved from farm to factory. To this internal migration was added the flood of foreign immigrants constituting the greatest migration in history, which crested in 1914 and transformed the ethnic character of the American population. After the war with Spain in 1898, the United States, with a large navy and extraterritorial possessions, emerged as a world power. Finally, the rise of universities during the latter part of the nineteenth century furnished not only a large number of centers of learning, laboratories for the advancement of science, but seedbeds for the dissemination of new social and political ideas (Selection 2). The confluence of these revolutionary developments brought about an intensification of the problems of human suffering and aroused concern and a consequent growing awareness that man could be free from disease, poverty, industrial accidents, and even manual labor, through the applications of science and technology. For example, knowledge of bacteriology, developed in the laboratories and classrooms of American universities and disseminated to the farm and the city through the United States Department of Agriculture and the public health movement, achieved dramatic successes in the conquest of diseases such as anthrax, diphtheria, and yellow fever.

The obstacle in the way of extending the bounds of freedom appeared to be economic individualism, bolstered by a restricted view of the role of government. The issue focused finally not on the question of whether the government had any responsibility for the social and economic welfare of its citizens, but on the question of just what the nature and extent of that responsibility was (Selection 3). The climax of the debate came with the presidential campaign of 1912, with Theodore Roosevelt propounding the tenets of his paternalistic New Nationalism (Selection 4) and Woodrow Wilson intoning the creed of the reactionary New Freedom (Selection 5). Resolution of the issue came when the Wilson administration, elected on the platform of the New Freedom, sought reelection on a record of enacting the principles of the New Nationalism. Only when the United States entered the First World War was the question of the status of individual rights within a national state raised anew.

1 / FREEDOM FOR INTELLIGENT ACTION

Born in Burlington, Vermont, in 1859, John Dewey attended the University of Vermont and received his Ph.D. in 1884 from Johns Hopkins University. For ten years he served as head of the philosophy department of the University of Chicago, where he established the first experimental school in the United States. He taught at Columbia University from 1904 until his retirement in 1929, after which he traveled, lectured, and wrote continuously until his death in 1952. Building on the work of Charles Peirce and William James, Dewey extended the philosophy of pragmatism to cover all aspects of life, calling his philosophy instrumentalism—a philosophy of action, not introspection. He inspired the progressive education movement and supplied a rationale for many of the progressive reformers. ¶Dewey wrote the essay that follows for a special American number of the French Revue de Métaphysique et de Morale *(October, 1922). Although not strictly within the chronological ordering of this book, the succinctness with which the selection conveys some of the most important new ideas of the beginning of the century justifies its placement at the beginning of the book.*

The purpose of this article is to define the principal theories of the philosophical movements known under the names of Pragmatism, Instrumentalism, or Experimentalism. To do this we must trace their historical development; for this method seems to present the simplest way of comprehending these movements and at the same

SOURCE: John Dewey, 'The Development of American Pragmatism," in *Studies in the History of Ideas*, II (New York: Columbia University Press, 1925), pp. 353-77.

time avoids certain current misunderstandings of their doctrines and of their aims.

The origin of Pragmatism goes back to Charles Sanders Peirce, the son of one of the most celebrated mathematicians of the United States, and himself very proficient in the science of mathematics; he is one of the founders of the modern symbolic logic of relations. Unfortunately Peirce was not at all a systematic writer and never expounded his ideas in a single system. The pragmatic method which he developed applies only to a very narrow and limited universe of discourse. After William James had extended the scope of the method, Peirce wrote an exposition of the origin of pragmatism as he had first conceived it; it is from this exposition that we take the following passages.

The term "pragmatic," contrary to the opinion of those who regard pragmatism as an exclusively American conception, was suggested to him by the study of Kant. In the "Metaphysic of Morals" Kant established a distinction between *pragmatic* and *practical*. The latter term applies to moral laws which Kant regards as *a priori,* whereas the former term applies to the rules of art and technique which are based on experience and are applicable to experience. Peirce, who was an empiricist, with the habits of mind, as he put it, of the laboratory, consequently refused to call his system "practicalism," as some of his friends suggested. As a logician he was interested in the art and technique of real thinking, and especially as far as pragmatic method is concerned in the art of making concepts clear, or of construing adequate and effective definitions in accord with the spirit of scientific method.

Following his own words, for a person "who still thought in Kantian terms most readily, *'praktisch'* and *'pragmatisch'* were as far apart as the two poles; the former belonging in a region of thought where no mind of the experimental type can ever make sure of solid ground under his feet, the latter expressing relation to some definite human purpose. Now quite the most striking feature of the new theory was its recognition of an inseparable connection between rational cognition and rational purpose." [1]

In alluding to the experimental type of mind, we are brought to the exact meaning given by Peirce to the word "pragmatic." In speaking of an experimentalist as a man whose intelligence is

[1] *Monist,* vol. 15, p. 163.

formed in the laboratory, he said: "Whatever assertion you may make to him, he will either understand as meaning that if a given prescription for an experiment ever can be and ever is carried out in act, an experience of a given description will result, else he will see no sense at all in what you say." And thus Peirce developed the theory that "the rational purport of a word or other expression, lies exclusively in its conceivable bearing upon the conduct of life; so that, since obviously nothing that might not result from experiment can have any direct bearing upon conduct, if one can define accurately all the conceivable experimental phenomena which the affirmation or denial of a concept could imply, one will have therein a complete definition of the concept." [2]

The essay in which Peirce developed his theory bears the title: *How to Make Our Ideas Clear.*[3] There is a remarkable similarity here to Kant's doctrine in the efforts which he made to interpret the universality of concepts in the domain of experience in the same way in which Kant established the law of practical reason in the domain of the *a priori.* "The rational meaning of every proposition lies in the future. . . . But of the myriads of forms into which a proposition may be translated, what is that one which is to be called its very meaning? It is, according to the pragmatist, that form in which the proposition becomes applicable to human conduct, not in these or those special circumstances, nor when one entertains this or that special design, but that form which is most directly applicable to self-control under every situation, and to every purpose." [4] So also, "the pragmatist does not make the *summum bonum* to consist in action, but makes it to consist in that process of evolution whereby the existent comes more and more to embody generals . . ." [5]—in other words—the process whereby the existent becomes, with the aid of action, a body of rational tendencies or of habits generalized as much as possible. These statements of Peirce are quite conclusive with respect to two errors which are commonly committed in regard to the ideas of the founder of pragmatism. It is often said of pragmatism that it makes action the end of life. It is also said of pragmatism that it subordinates thought and rational activity to particular ends of interest and profit. It is true that the theory according to Peirce's conception implies essentially

[2] *Monist,* vol. 15, p. 162.   [3] *Popular Science Monthly,* 1878.
[4] *Monist,* vol. 15, pp. 173-4.   [5] *Monist,* vol. 15, p. 178.

a certain relation to action, to human conduct. But the rôle of action is that of an intermediary. In order to be able to attribute a meaning to concepts, one must be able to apply them to existence. Now it is by means of action that this application is made possible. And the modification of existence which results from this application constitutes the true meaning of concepts.

Pragmatism is, therefore, far from being that glorification of action for its own sake which is regarded as the peculiar characteristic of American life. It is also to be noted that there is a scale of possible applications of concepts to existence, and hence a diversity of meanings. The greater the extension of the concepts, the more they are freed from the restrictions which limit them to particular cases, the more is it possible for us to attribute the most general meaning to a term. Thus the theory of Peirce is opposed to every restriction of the meaning of a concept to the achievement of a particular end, and still more to a personal aim. It is still more strongly opposed to the idea that reason or thought should be reduced to being a servant of any interest which is pecuniary or too narrow. This theory was American in its origin in so far as it insisted on the necessity of human conduct and the fulfillment of some aim in order to clarify thought. But at the same time, it disapproves of those aspects of American life which make action an end in itself, and which conceive ends too narrowly and too practically. In considering a system of philosophy in its relation to national factors it is necessary to keep in mind not only the aspects of life which are incorporated in the system, but also the aspects against which the system is a protest. There never was a philosopher who has merited the name for the simple reason that he glorified the tendencies and characteristics of his social environment; just as it is also true that there never has been a philosopher who has not seized upon certain aspects of the life of his time and idealized them.

The work commenced by Peirce was continued by William James. In one sense James narrowed the application of Peirce's pragmatic method, but at the same time he extended it. The articles which Peirce wrote in 1878 commanded almost no attention from philosophical circles, which were then under the dominating influence of the neo-kantian idealism of Green, of Caird, and of the Oxford School, excepting those circles in which the Scottish philosophy of common sense maintained its supremacy. In 1898 James inaugurated the new pragmatic movement in an address entitled, "Philosophical Conceptions and Practical Results," later reprinted in the volume, *Collected Essays and Reviews*. Even in this early study one can easily notice the presence of those two tendencies to restrict and at the same time to extend early pragmatism. After having quoted the psychological remark of Peirce that "beliefs are really rules for action, and the whole function of thinking is but one step in the production of habits of action," and that every idea which we frame for ourselves of an object is really an idea of the possible effects of that object, he expressed the opinion that all these principles could be expressed more broadly than Peirce expressed them.

The ultimate test for us of what a truth means is indeed the conduct it dictates or inspires. But it inspires that conduct because it first foretells some particular turn to our experience which shall call for just that conduct from us. And I should prefer to express Peirce's principle by saying that the effective meaning of any philosophic proposition can always be brought down to some particular consequence, in our future practical experience, whether active or passive; the point lying rather in the fact that the experience must be particular, than in the fact that it must be active.[6]

In an essay written in 1908 James repeats this statement and states that whenever he employs the term "the practical," he means by it, "the distinctively concrete, the individual, the particular and effective as opposed to the abstract, general and inert—'Pragmata' are things in their plurality—particular consequences can perfectly well be of a theoretic nature." [7] [8]

[6] *Collected Essays and Reviews*, p. 412.   [7] *The Meaning of Truth*, pp. 209-210.
[8] In a footnote James gave an example of the errors which are committed in connection with the term "Practical," quoting M. Bourdeau who had written that "Pragmatism is an Anglo Saxon reaction against the intellectualism and nationalism of the Latin mind. . . . It is a philosophy without words, a philosophy of gestures and of facts, which abandons what is general and holds only to what is particular." In his lecture at California, James brought out the idea that his pragmatism was inspired to a considerable extent by the thought of the British philosophers, Locke, Berkeley, Hume, Mill, Bain, and Shadworth Hodgson. But he contrasted this method with German transcendentalism, and particularly with that of Kant. It is especially interesting to notice this differ-

William James alluded to the development which he gave to Peirce's expression of the principle. In one sense one can say that he enlarged the bearing of the principle by the substitution of particular consequences for the general rule or method applicable to future experience. But in another sense this substitution limited the application of the principle since it destroyed the importance attached by Peirce to the greatest possible application of the rule, or the habit of conduct—its extension to universality. That is to say, William James was much more of a nominalist than Peirce.

One can notice an extension of pragmatism in the above passage. James there alludes to the use of a method of determining the meaning of truth. Since truth is a term and has consequently a meaning, this extension is a legitimate application of pragmatic method. But it should be remarked that here this method serves only to make clear the meaning of the term, and has nothing to do with the truth of a particular judgment. The principal reason which led James to give a new color to pragmatic method was that he was preoccupied with applying the method to determine the meaning of philosophical problems and questions and that moreover, he chose to submit to examination philosophical notions of a theological or religious nature. He wished to establish a criterion which would enable one to determine whether a given philosophical question has an authentic and vital meaning or whether, on the contrary, it was trivial and purely verbal; and in the former case, what interests were at stake, when one accepts and affirms one or the other of two theses in dispute. Peirce was above all a logician; whereas James was an educator and wished to force the general public to realize that certain problems, certain philosophical debates have a real importance for mankind, because the beliefs which they bring into play lead to very different modes of conduct. If this important distinction is not grasped, it is impossible to understand the majority of the ambiguities and errors which belong to the later period in the pragmatic movement.

James took as an example the controversy between theism and materialism. It follows from this principle that if the course of the

---

ence between Peirce and James: the former attempted to give an experimental, not an *a priori* explanation of Kant, whereas James tried to develop the point of view of the British thinkers.

world is considered as completed, it is equally legitimate to assert that God or matter was its cause. Whether one way or the other, the facts are what they are, and it is they which determine whatever meaning is to be given to their cause. Consequently the name which we can give to this cause is entirely arbitrary. It is entirely different if we take the future into account. God then has the meaning of a power concerned with assuring the final triumph of ideal and spiritual values, and matter becomes a power indifferent to the triumph or defeat of these values. And our life takes a different direction according as we adopt one or the other of these alternatives. In the lectures on pragmatism published in 1907, he applies the same criticism to the philosophical problem of the One and the Many, that is to say of Monism and Pluralism, as well as to other questions. Thus he shows that Monism is equivalent to a rigid universe where everything is fixed and immutably united to others, where indetermination, free choice, novelty, and the unforeseen in experience have no place; a universe which demands the sacrifice of the concrete and complex diversity of things to the simplicity and nobility of an architectural structure. In what concerns our beliefs, Monism demands a rationalistic temperament leading to a fixed and dogmatic attitude. Pluralism, on the other hand, leaves room for contingence, liberty, novelty, and gives complete liberty of action to the empirical method, which can be greatly extended. It accepts unity where it finds it, but it does not attempt to force the vast diversity of events and things into a single rational mold.

From the point of view of an educator or of a student or, if you will, of those who are thoroughly interested in these problems, in philosophical discussions and controversies, there is no reason for contesting the value of this application of pragmatic method, but it is no less important to determine the nature of this application. It affords a means of discovering the implications for human life of philosophical conceptions which are often treated as of no importance and of a purely dialectical nature. It furnishes a criterion for determining the vital implications of beliefs which present themselves as alternatives in any theory. Thus as he himself said, "the whole function of philosophy ought to be to find the characteristic influences which you and I would undergo at a determinate moment of our lives, if one or the other formula of the universe were true." However, in saying that the whole function of philosophy has this aim, it seems that he is referring rather to the teaching than to the construction of philosophy. For such a statement implies that the world formulas have already all been made, and that the necessary work of producing them has already been finished, so that there remains only to define the consequences which are reflected in life by the acceptance of one or the other of these formulas as true.

From the point of view of Peirce, the object of philosophy would be rather to give a fixed meaning to the universe by formulas which correspond to our attitudes or our most general habits of response to the environment; and this generality depends on the extension of the applicability of these formulas to specific future events. The meaning of concepts of "matter" and of "God" must be fixed before we can even attempt to reach an understanding concerning the value of our belief in these terms. Materialism would signify that the world demands on our part a single kind of constant and general habits; and God would signify the demand for another type of habits; the difference between materialism and theism would be tantamount to the difference in the habits required to face all the detailed facts of the universe. The world would be one in so far as it would be possible for us to form a single habit of action which would take account of all future existences and would be applicable to them. It would be many in so far as it is necessary for us to form several habits, differing from each other and irreducible to each other, in order to be able to meet the events in the world and control them. In short, Peirce wrote as a logician and James as a humanist.

William James accomplished a new advance in Pragmatism by his theory of the will to believe, or as he himself later called it, the right to believe. The discovery of the fundamental consequences of one or another belief has without fail a certain influence on that belief itself. If a man cherished novelty, risk, opportunity and a variegated esthetic reality, he will certainly reject any belief in Monism, when he clearly perceives the import of this system. But if, from the very start, he is attracted by esthetic harmony, classic proportions, fixity even to the extent of absolute security and logical coherence, it is quite natural that he should put faith in Monism. Thus William James took into account those motives of instinctive sympathy which play a greater rôle in our choice of a philosophic system than formal reasonings; and he thought that we would be rendering a service to the cause of philosophical sincerity if we would openly recognize the motives which inspire us. He also maintained the thesis that the greater part of philosophic problems and especially those which touch on religious fields are of such a nature that they are not susceptible of decisive evidence one way or the other. Consequently he claimed the right of a man to choose his beliefs not only in the presence of proofs or conclusive facts, but also in the absence of all evidence of this nature, and above all when he is forced to choose between one meaning or another, or when by refusing to choose, his refusal is itself equivalent to a choice. The theory of the will to believe gives rise to misunderstandings and even to ridicule; and therefore it is necessary to understand clearly in what way James used it. We are always obliged to act in any case; our actions and with them their consequences actually change according to the beliefs which we have chosen. Moreover it may be that, in order to discover the proofs which will ultimately be the intellectual justification of certain beliefs—the belief in freedom, for example, or the belief in God—it is necessary to begin to act in accordance with this belief.

In his lectures on Pragmatism, and in his volume of essays bearing the title *The Meaning of Truth*, which appeared in 1909, James extended the use of the pragmatic method to the problem of the nature of truth. So far we have considered the pragmatic method as an instrument in determining the meaning of words and the vital importance of philosophic beliefs. Now and then we have made allusion to the future consequences which are implied. James showed, among other things, that in certain philosophic conceptions, the affirmation of certain beliefs could be justified by means of the nature of their consequences, or by the differences which these beliefs make in existence. But then why not push the argument to the point of maintaining that the meaning of truth in general is determined by its consequences? We must not forget here that James was an empiricist before he was a pragmatist, and repeatedly stated that pragmatism is merely empiricism pushed to its legitimate conclusions. From a general point of view, the pragmatic attitude consists in "looking away from first things, principles, 'categories,' supposed necessities; and of looking towards last things, fruits, consequences, facts." It is only one step further to apply the pragmatic method to the problem of truth. In the natural sciences there is a tendency to identify truth in any particular case with a verification. The verification of a theory, or of a concept, is carried on by the observation of particular facts. Even the most scientific and harmonious physical theory is merely an hypothesis until its implications, deduced by mathematical reasoning or by any other kind of inference, are verified by observed facts. What direction therefore, must an empirical philosopher take who wishes to arrive at a definition of truth by means of an empirical method? He must, if he wants to apply this method, and without bringing in for the present the pragmatic formula, first find particular cases from which he then generalizes. It is therefore in submitting conceptions to the control of experience, in the process of verifying them, that one finds examples of what is called truth. Therefore the philosopher who applies this empirical method, without the least prejudice in favor of pragmatic doctrine, can be brought to conclude that truth "means" verification, or if one prefers, that verification either actual or possible, is the definition of truth.

In combining this conception of empirical method with the theory of pragmatism, we come upon other important philosophical results. The classic theories of truth in terms of the coherence or compatibility of terms, and of the correspondence of an idea with a thing, hereby receive a new interpretation. A merely mental coherence without experimental verification does not enable us to get beyond the realm of hypothesis. If a notion or a theory makes pretense of corresponding to reality or to the facts, this pretense cannot be put to the test and confirmed or refuted except by causing it to pass over into the realm of action and by noting the results which it yields in the form of the concrete observable facts to which this notion or theory leads. If, in acting upon this notion, we are brought to the fact which it implies or which it demands, then this notion is true. A theory corresponds to the facts because it leads to the facts which are its consequences, by the intermediary of experience. And from this consideration the pragmatic generalization is drawn that all knowledge is prospective in its results, except in the case where notions and theories after having been first prospective in their application, have already been tried out and verified. Theoretically, however, even such verifications or truths could not be absolute. They would be based upon practical or moral certainty, but they are always subject to being corrected by unforeseen future consequences or by observed facts which had been disregarded. Every proposition concerning truths is really in the last analysis hypothetical and provisional, although a large number of these propositions have been so frequently verified without fail that we are justified in using them as if they were absolutely true. But logically absolute truth is an ideal which cannot be realized, at least not until all the facts have been registered, or as James says "bagged," and until it is no longer possible to make other observations and other experiences.

Pragmatism, thus, presents itself as an extension of historical empiricism with this fundamental difference, that it does not insist upon antecedent phenomena but upon consequent phenomena; not upon the precedents but upon the possibilities of action, and this change in point of view is almost revolutionary in its consequences. An empiricism which is content with repeating facts already past has no place for possibility and for liberty. It cannot find room for general conceptions or ideas, at least no more than to consider them as summaries or records. But when we take the point of view of pragmatism we see that general ideas have a very different rôle to play than that of reporting and registering past experiences. They are the bases for organizing future observations and experiences. Whereas, for empiricism, in a world already constructed and determined, reason or general thought has no other meaning than that of summing up particular cases, in a world where the future is not a mere word, where theories, general notions, rational ideas have consequences for action, reason necessarily has a constructive function. Nevertheless the conceptions of reasoning have only a secondary interest in comparison with the reality of facts, since they must be confronted with concrete observations.[9]

Pragmatism thus has a metaphysical implication. The doctrine

[9] William James said in a happy metaphor, that they must be "cashed in," by producing specific consequences. This expression means that they must be able to become concrete facts. But for those who are not familiar with American idioms, James' formula was taken to mean that the consequences themselves of our rational conceptions must be narrowly limited by their pecuniary value. Thus Mr. Bertrand Russell wrote just recently that pragmatism is merely a manifestation of American commercialism.

of the value of consequences leads us to take the future into consideration. And this taking into consideration of the future takes us to the conception of a universe whose evolution is not finished, of a universe which is still, in James' term, "in the making," "in the process of becoming," of a universe up to a certain point still plastic.

Consequently reason, or thought, in its more general sense, has a real, though limited function, a creative, constructive function. If we form general ideas and if we put them in action, consequences are produced which could not be produced otherwise. Under these conditions the world will be different from what it would have been if thought had not intervened. This consideration confirms the human and moral importance of thought and of its reflective operation in experience. It is therefore not true to say that James treated reason, thought and knowledge with contempt, or that he regarded them as mere means of gaining personal or even social profits. For him reason has a creative function, limited because specific, which helps to make the world other than it would have been without it. It makes the world really more reasonable; it gives to it an intrinsic value. One will understand the philosophy of James better if one considers it in its totality as a revision of English empiricism, a revision which replaces the value of past experience, of what is already given, by the future, by that which is mere possibility.

These considerations naturally bring us to the movement called instrumentalism. The survey which we have just made of James' philosophy shows that he regarded conceptions and theories purely as instruments which can serve to constitute future facts in a specific manner. But James devoted himself primarily to the moral aspects of this theory, to the support which it gave to "meliorism" and moral idealism, and to the consequences which followed from it concerning the sentimental value and the bearing of various philosophical systems, particularly to its destructive implications for monistic rationalism and for absolutism in all its forms. He never attempted to develop a complete theory of the forms or "structures" and of the logical operations which are founded on this conception. Instrumentalism is an attempt to constitute a precise logical theory of concepts, of judgments and inferences in their various forms, by considering primarily how thought functions in the experimental determinations of future consequences. That is to say, that it attempts to establish universally recognized distinctions and rules of logic by deriving them from the reconstructive or mediative function ascribed to reason. It aims to constitute a theory of the general forms of conception and reasoning, and not of this or that particular judgment or concept related to its own content, or to its particular implications.

As far as the historical antecedents of instrumentalism are concerned, two factors are particularly important, over and above this matter of experimental verification which we have already mentioned in connection with James. The first of these two factors is psychological, and the second is a critique of the theory of knowledge and of logic which has resulted from the theory proposed by neo-kantian idealism and expounded in the logical writings of such philosophers as Lotze, Bosanquet, and F. H. Bradley. As we have already said, neo-kantian influence was very marked in the United States during the last decade of the nineteenth century. I myself, and those who have collaborated with me in the exposition of instrumentalism, began by being neo-kantians, in the same way that Peirce's point of departure was kantianism and that of James was the empiricism of the British School.

The psychological tendencies which have exerted an influence on instrumentalism are of a biological rather than a physiological nature. They are closely related to the important movement whose promoter in psychology has been Doctor John Watson and to which he has given the name of Behaviourism. Briefly, the point of departure of this theory is the conception of the brain as an organ for the co-ordination of sense stimuli (to which one should add modifications caused by habit, unconscious memory, or what are called today "conditioned reflexes") for the purpose of effecting appropriate motor responses. On the basis of the theory of organic evolution it is maintained that the analysis of intelligence and of its operations should be compatible with the order of known biological facts, concerning the intermediate position occupied by the central nervous system in making possible responses to the environment adequate to the needs of the living organism. It is particularly interesting to note that in the *Studies in Logical Theory* (1903), which was their first declaration, the instrumentalists recognized how much they owed to William James for having forged the instruments which they used, while at the same time, in the course of the studies, the authors constantly declared their belief in a close union of the "normative" principles of logic and the real processes of thought, in so far as these are determined by an objective or biological psychology and not by an introspective psychology of states of consciousness. But it is curious to note that the "instruments" to which allusion is made, are not the considerations which were of the greatest service to James. They precede his pragmatism and it is in one of the aspects of his *Principles of Psychology* that one must look for them. This important work (1890) really developed two distinct theses.

The one is a re-interpretation of introspective psychology, in which James denies that sensations, images and ideas are discreet and in which he replaces them by a continuous stream which he calls "the stream of consciousness." This conception necessitates a consideration of relations as an immediate part of the field of consciousness, having the same status as qualities. And throughout his *Psychology* James gives a philosophical tinge to this conception by using it in criticising the atomism of Locke and of Hume as well as the a-priorism of the synthesis of rational principles by Kant and his successors, among whom should be mentioned in England, Thomas Hill Green, who was then at the height of his influence.

The other aspect of his *Principles of Psychology* is of a biological nature. It shows itself in its full force in the criterion which James established for discovering the existence of mind. "The pursuance of future ends and the choice of means for their attainment are thus the mark and criterion of the presence of mentality in a phenomenon." [10] The force of this criterion is plainly shown in the chapter on Attention, and its relation to Interest considered as the force which controls it, and its teleological function of selection and integration; in the chapter on Discrimination and Comparison (Analysis and Abstraction), where he discusses the way in which ends to be attained and the means for attaining them evoke and control intellectual analysis; and in the chapter on Conception, where he shows that a general idea is a mode of signifying particular things and not merely an abstraction from particular cases or a super-empirical function,—that it is a teleological instrument. James then develops this idea in the chapter on reasoning where he says that "the only meaning of essence is teleological, and that

[10] *Psychology*, vol. I, p. 8.

classification and conception are purely teleological weapons of mind."

One might complete this brief enumeration by mentioning also the chapter of James' book in which he discusses the Nature of Necessary Truths and the Rôle of Experience, and affirms in opposition to Herbert Spencer, that many of our most important modes of perception and conception of the world of sensible objects are not the cumulative products of particular experience, but rather original biological sports, spontaneous variations which are maintained because of their applicability to concrete experiences after once having been created. Number, space, time, resemblance and other important "categories" could have been brought into existence, he says, as a consequence of some particular cerebral instability, but they could by no means have been registered by the mind under some outside influence. Many significant and useless concepts also arise in the same manner. But the fundamental categories have been cumulatively extended and reinforced because of their value when applied to concrete instances and things of experience. It is therefore not the origin of a concept, it is its application which becomes the criterion of its value; and here we have the whole of pragmatism in embryo. A phrase of James' very well summarizes its import: "the popular notion that 'Science' is forced on the mind ab extra, and that our interests have nothing to do with its constructions, is utterly absurd."

Given the point of view which we have just specified, and the interest attaching to a logical theory of conception and judgment, there results a theory of the following description. The adaptations made by inferior organisms, for example their effective and coordinated responses to stimuli, become teleological in man and therefore give occasion to thought. Reflection is an indirect response to the environment, and the element of indirection can itself become great and very complicated. But it has its origin in biological adaptive behaviour and its ultimate function in its cognitive aspect is a prospective control of the conditions of its environment. The function of intelligence is therefore not that of copying the objects of the environment, but rather of taking account of the way in which more effective and more profitable relations with these objects may be established in the future.

How this point of view has been applied to the theory of judgment is too long a story to be told here. We shall confine ourselves here to saying that, in general, the "subject" of a judgment represents that portion of the environment to which a reaction must be made; the attribute represents the corresponding response or the habit or the manner in which one must behave towards the environment; the copula represents the organic and concrete act by which the connection is made between the fact and its signification; and finally the conclusion, or the definitive object of judgment, is simply the same situation transformed, a situation which implies a change as well in the original subject (including its mind) as in the environment itself. The new and harmonious unity thus attained verifies the bearing of the data which were at first chosen to serve as subject and of the concepts introduced into the situation during the process as teleological instruments for its elaboration. Until this final unification is attained the perceptual data and the conceptual principles, theories, are merely hypotheses from a logical point of view. Moreover, affirmation and negation are intrinsically a-logical: they are acts.

Such a summary survey can hardly pretend to be either convincing or suggestive. However, in noting the points of resemblance and difference between this phase of pragmatism and the logic of neo-hegelian idealism, we are bringing out a point of great importance. According to the latter logic, thought constitutes in the last analysis its own object and even the universe. It is possible to affirm the existence of a series of forms of judgment, because our first judgments, which are nearest to sense, succeed in constituting objects in only a partial and fragmentary fashion, even to the extent of involving in their nature an element of contradiction. There results a dialectic which permits each inferior and partial type of judgment to pass into a more complete form until we finally arrive at the total judgment where the thought which comprehends the entire object or the universe as an organic whole of interrelated mental distinctions. It is evident that this theory magnifies the rôle of thought beyond all proportion. It is an objective and rational idealism which is opposed to and distinct from the subjective and perceptual idealism of Berkeley's school. Instrumentalism, however, assigns a positive function to thought, that of reconstituting the present stage of things instead of merely knowing them. As a consequence, there cannot be intrinsic degrees, or a hierarchy of forms of judgment. Each type has its own end, and its validity is entirely determined by its efficacy in the pursuit of its end. A limited perceptual judgment, adapted to the situation which has given it birth, is as true as is the most complete and significant philosophic or scientific judgment in its place. Logic, therefore, leads to a realistic metaphysics in so far as it accepts facts and events for what they are independently of thought, and to an idealistic metaphysics in so far as it contends that thought gives birth to distinctive acts which modify future facts and events in such a way as to render them more reasonable, that is to say, more adequate to the ends which we propose for ourselves. The ideal element is more accentuated by the inclusion progressively of social factors in human environment over and above natural factors; so that the needs which are fulfilled, the ends which are attained are no longer of a merely biological or particular character, but include also the ends and activities of other members of society.

It is natural that continental thinkers should be interested in American philosophy as it reflects, in a certain sense, American life. Thus it is clear after this rapid survey of the history of pragmatism that American thought merely continues European thought. We have imported our language, our laws, our institutions, our morals, and our religion from Europe, and we have adapted them to the new conditions of our life. The same is true of our ideas. For long years our philosophical thought was merely an echo of European thought. The pragmatic movement which we have traced in the present essay as well as neo-realism, behaviourism, the absolute idealism of Royce, the naturalistic idealism of Santayana, are all attempts at re-adaptation; but they are not creations *de novo*. They have their roots in British and European thought. Since these systems are re-adaptations they take into consideration the distinctive traits of the environment of American life. But as has already been said, they are not limited to reproducing what is worn and imperfect in this environment. They do not aim to glorify the energy and the love of action which the new conditions of American life exaggerated. They do not reflect the excessive mercantilism of American life. Without doubt all these traits of the environment have not been without a certain influence on American philosophical thought; our philosophy would not be national or spontaneous if it were not subject to this influence. But the fundamental idea

which the movements of which we have just spoken, have attempted to express, is the idea that action and opportunity justify
themselves only to the degree in which they render life more reasonable and increase its value. Instrumentalism maintains in opposition to many contrary tendencies in the American environment,
that action should be intelligent and reflective, and that thought
should occupy a central position in life. That is the reason for our
insistence on the teleological phase of thought and knowledge. If it
must be teleological in particular and not merely true in the abstract that is probably due to the practical element which is found
in all the phases of American life. However that may be, what we
insist upon above all else is that intelligence be regarded as the
only source and sole guarantee of a desirable and happy future.
It is beyond doubt that the progressive and unstable character of
American life and civilization has facilitated the birth of a philosophy which regards the world as being in continuous formation,
where there is still place for indeterminism, for the new and for a
real future. But this idea is not exclusively American, although the
conditions of American life have aided this idea in becoming self-
conscious. It is also true that Americans tend to underestimate the
value of tradition and of rationality considered as an achievement
of the past. But the world has also given proof of irrationality in
the past and this irrationality is incorporated in our beliefs and our
institutions. There are bad traditions as there are good ones: it is
always important to distinguish. Our neglect of the traditions of
the past, with whatever this negligence implies in the way of spiritual impoverishment of our life, has its compensation in the idea
that the world is re-commencing and being re-made under our eyes.
The future as well as the past can be a source of interest and consolation and give meaning to the present. Pragmatism and instrumental experimentalism bring into prominence the importance of
the individual. It is he who is the carrier of creative thought, the
author of action, and of its application. Subjectivism is an old story
in philosophy; a story which began in Europe and not in America.
But American philosophy, in the systems which we have expounded,
has given to the subject, to the individual mind, a practical rather
than an epistemological function. The individual mind is important
because only the individual mind is the organ of modifications in
traditions and institutions, the vehicle of experimental creation.

One-sided and egoistic individualism in American life has left its imprint in our thought. For better or for worse, depending on the point of view, it has transformed the esthetic and fixed individualism of the old European culture into an active individualism. But the idea of a society of individuals is not foreign to American thought; it penetrates even our current individualism which is unreflective and brutal. And the individual which American thought idealises is not an individual *per se*, an individual fixed in isolation and set up for himself, but an individual who evolves and develops in a natural and human environment, an individual who can be educated.

If I were asked to give an historical parallel to this movement in American thought I would remind my reader of the French philosophy of the enlightenment. Everyone knows that the thinkers who made that movement illustrious were inspired by Bacon, Locke, and Newton; what interested them was the application of scientific method and of the conclusions of an experimental theory of knowledge to human affairs, the critique and reconstruction of beliefs and institutions. As Höffding writes, they were animated "by a fervent faith in intelligence, progress, and humanity." And certainly they are not accused today, just because of their educational and social significance, of having sought to subordinate intelligence and science to ordinary utilitarian aims. They merely sought to free intelligence from its impurities and to render it sovereign. One can scarcely say that those who glorify intelligence and reason in the abstract, because of their value for those who find personal satisfaction in their possession, estimate intelligence more truly than those who wish to make it the sole and indispensable guide of intellectual and social life. When an American critic says of instrumentalism that it regards ideas as mere servants which make for success in life, he need only react, without reflection, on the ordinary verbal associations of the word "instrumental," as many others have reacted in the same manner to the use of the word "practical." Similarly a recent Italian writer after having said that pragmatism and instrumentalism are characteristic products of American thought, adds that these systems "regard intelligence as a mere mechanism of belief, and consequently attempt to re-establish the dignity of reason by making of it a machine for the production of beliefs useful to morals and society." This criticism does not hold.

It is by no means the production of beliefs useful to morals and society which these systems pursue, but it is the formation of a faith in intelligence, as the one and indispensable belief necessary to moral and social life. The more one appreciates the intrinsic esthetic, immediate value of thought and of science, the more one takes into account what intelligence itself adds to the joy and dignity of life, the more one should feel grieved at a situation in which the exercise and joy of reason are limited to a narrow, closed and technical social group and the more one should ask how it is possible to make all participators in this inestimable wealth.

2 / THE CONSTITUTION: A NEW VIEW

J. Allen Smith, a political scientist, was born on the eve of the Civil War in 1860, in the border state of Missouri, and grew up amidst the bitter political and social upheavals of the Civil War and Reconstruction. He attended the University of Missouri, graduated in 1886, and went on to law school. During his college years he fell under the influence of Henry George after reading Progress and Poverty. *He took his Ph.D. in political science and economics at the University of Michigan in 1894, and in 1896 published his dissertation, "Multiple Money Standard," in the* Annals of the American Academy of Political and Social Science. *The essay was a theoretical study of money which refuted many of the contentions of the gold standard advocates and therefore almost inevitably figured in the bitter monetary discussions of the presidential campaign of 1896. As a result he was dropped from his job on the faculty at Marietta College the following year and became professor of political science at the University of Washington,*

SOURCE: J. Allen Smith, "Individual Liberty and the Constitution," Chapter XI in *The Spirit of American Government: A Study of the Constitution: Its Origin, Influence and Relation to Democracy* (New York & London: The Macmillan Company, 1912), pp. 292-303.

where he remained until his death in 1924. ¶In 1907,
Smith published The Spirit of American Government,
from which the following selection is taken. The
book, the first progressive attack on the old view
of the Constitution, presents the underlying principles of
American government, pointing out the undemocratic
features and the general confusion and irresponsibility
of political parties. Smith's work and ideas influenced not
only Theodore Roosevelt and Robert M. LaFollette, but
Charles A. Beard and Vernon Louis Parrington. The
controversy resulting from the book not only threatened
his job but made him sufficiently prominent that he was
asked to run for the Progressive nomination for governor
of the state of Washington in 1912, an offer he refused.

The American revolution, which supplanted hereditary by popular
rule, worked a fundamental change in the relation of the individual
to the government. So far at least as the voters were concerned the
government was no longer an alien institution—an authority imposed upon them from above, but an organization emanating from
them—one in which they had and felt a direct proprietary interest.
It was no longer a government in which the active principle was
irresponsible authority, but one which rested upon the safe and
trustworthy basis of popular control.

The overthrow of monarchy and aristocracy necessitated a corresponding change in the idea of liberty to make it fit the new
political conditions which had emerged. In so far as government
had now passed into the hands of the people there was no longer
any reason to fear that it would encroach upon what they regarded
as their rights. With the transition, then, from class to popular
sovereignty there was a corresponding change in the attitude of
the people toward the government. They naturally desired to limit
the authority and restrict the activity of the government as long as
they felt that it was irresponsible; but as soon as they acquired an
active control over it, the reason which formerly actuated them in
desiring to limit its powers was no longer operative. Their ends
could now be accomplished and their interests best furthered by
unhampered political activity. They would now desire to remove

the checks upon the government for the same reason that they formerly sought to impose them—viz., to promote their own welfare.

This tendency is seen in the changes made in the state constitutions at the beginning of the American revolution. . . . They established the supremacy of the legislative body and through this branch of the government, the supremacy of the majority of the qualified voters. We have here a new conception of liberty. We see a tendency in these constitutional changes to reject the old passive view of state interference as limited by the consent of the governed and take the view that real liberty implies much more than the mere power of constitutional resistance—that it is something positive, that its essence is the power to actively control and direct the policy of the state. The early state constitutions thus represent a long step in the direction of unlimited responsible government.

This, as we have seen, was the chief danger which the conservative classes saw in the form of government established at the outbreak of the Revolution. They were afraid that the power of the numerical majority would be employed to further the interests of the many at the expense of the few, and to guard against such a use of the government they sought to re-establish the system of checks. The Constitution which restored the old scheme of government in a new garb also revived the old conception of individual liberty. There is, however, one important difference between the eighteenth-century conception of liberty and that which finds expression in our constitutional literature. Formerly it was because of the lack of popular control that the people generally desired to limit the authority of the government, but the framers of the Constitution wished to bring about the limitation of governmental functions because they feared the consequences of majority rule. Formerly the many advocated the limitation of the power of king and aristocracy in the interest of liberty; now the few advocate the limitation of the power of the many for their own protection. With the abolition of monarchy and aristocracy the attitude of the few and the many has been reversed. The aristocratic and special interests that formerly opposed the limitation of political activity when they were predominant in the government, now favor it as a protection against the growing power of the masses, while the latter, who formerly favored, now oppose it. The conservative classes now regard the popular majority with the same distrust which the liberals formerly felt toward the king and aristocracy. In fact, the present-day conservative goes even farther than this and would have us believe that the popular major.ty is a much greater menace to liberty than king or aristocracy has ever been in the past.

"There can be no tyranny of a monarch so intolerable," says a recent American writer, "as that of the multitude, for it has the power behind it that no king can sway." [1] This is and has all along been the attitude of the conservative classes who never lose an opportunity to bring the theory of democracy into disrepute. The defenders of the American Constitution clearly see that unless the fundamental principle of popular government is discredited the system of checks can not survive.

There is no liberty, we are told by the present-day followers of Alexander Hamilton, where the majority is supreme. The American political system realizes this conception of liberty mainly through the Supreme Court—an organ of government which interprets the Constitution and laws of Congress and which may forbid the carrying out of the expressed will of the popular majority. It necessarily follows that the authority which can thus overrule the majority and enforce its own views of the system is an authority greater than the majority. All governments must belong to one or the other of two classes according as the ultimate basis of political power is the many or the few. There is, in fact, no middle ground. We must either recognize the many as supreme, with no checks upon their authority except such as are implied in their own intelligence, sense of justice and spirit of fair play, or we must accept the view that the ultimate authority is in the hands of the few. Every scheme under which the power of the majority is limited means in its practical operation the subordination of the majority to the minority. This inevitable consequence of the limitation of popular rule is not alluded to by the advocates of checks and balances, though it is obvious to any careful student of the system.

It would, however, do injustice to the intelligence of those who champion the scheme of checks and balances to give them credit

[1] W. W. Willoughby, *An Examination of the Nature of the State* (New York, 1896), p. 416.

for any real sympathy with the aims and purposes of democracy. Individual liberty as guaranteed by majority rule was not the end which the framers of the Constitution had in view, nor is it the reason why the present-day conservative defends their work. The Constitution as originally adopted did not contain that highly prized guarantee of personal liberty which democracy everywhere insists upon. The failure to make any provision for freedom of the press should be regarded as a significant omission. This, however, was not an essential part of the Federalists' scheme of government, which aimed rather to protect the property and privileges of the few than to guarantee personal liberty to the masses. This omission is the more noteworthy in view of the fact that this guarantee was at that time expressly included in a majority of the state constitutions, and that the temper of the people was such as to compel its speedy adoption as an amendment to the Federal Constitution itself.

Liberty, as the framers of the Constitution understood the term, had to do primarily with property and property rights. The chief danger which they saw in the Revolutionary state governments was the opportunity afforded to the majority to legislate upon matters which the well-to-do classes wished to place beyond the reach of popular interference. The unlimited authority which the state government had over taxation and its power to restrict or abridge property rights were viewed with alarm by the wealthy classes, who felt that any considerable measure of democracy would be likely to deprive them of their time-honored prerogatives. To guard against this danger the Constitution sought, in the interest of the classes which dominated the Federal Convention, to give the widest possible scope to private property. It prohibited private property in nothing—permitting it, as originally adopted, even in human beings. It may be said without exaggeration that the American scheme of government was planned and set up to perpetuate the ascendency of the property-holding class in a society leavened with democratic ideas. Those who framed it were fully alive to the fact that their economic advantages could be retained only by maintaining their class ascendency in the government. They understood the economic significance of democracy. They realized that if the supremacy of the majority were once fully established the entire policy of the government would be profoundly changed.

They foresaw that it would mean the abolition of all private monopoly and the abridgment and regulation of property rights in the interest of the general public.

The Constitution was in form a political document, but its significance was mainly economic. It was the outcome of an organized movement on the part of a class to surround themselves with legal and constitutional guarantees which would check the tendency toward democratic legislation. These were made effective through the attitude of the United States courts which, as Professor Burgess says, "have never declined jurisdiction where private property was immediately affected on the ground that the question was political." [2]

"There can be no question that the national government has given to the minority a greater protection than it has enjoyed anywhere else in the world, save in those countries where the minority is a specially privileged aristocracy and the right of suffrage is limited. So absolute have property rights been held by the Supreme Court, that it even, by the Dred Scott decision, in effect made the whole country a land of slavery, because the slave was property, and the rights of property were sacred." [3]

In carrying out the original intent of the Constitution with reference to property the courts have developed and applied the doctrine of vested rights—a doctrine which has been used with telling effect for the purpose of defeating democratic reforms. This doctrine briefly stated is that property rights once granted are sacred and inviolable. A rigid adherence to this policy would effectually deprive the government of the power to make the laws governing private property conform to social and economic changes. It would disregard the fact that vested rights are often vested wrongs, and that one important, if not indeed the most important, task which a government by and for the people has to perform is to rectify past mistakes and correct the evils growing out of corruption and class rule. A government without authority to interfere with vested rights would have little power to promote the general welfare through legislation.

The adoption of the Constitution brought this doctrine from the

[2] John W. Burgess, *Political Science and Comparative Constitutional Law*, (Boston, 1890), I, 197.

[3] P. L. Ford, ed., *The Federalist* (New York, 1898), Introduction, p. xiii.

realm of political speculation into the arena of practical politics. The men who framed and set up our Federal government were shrewd enough to see that if the interests of the property-holding classes were to be given effective protection, it was necessary that political power should rest ultimately upon a class basis. This they expected to accomplish largely through the judicial veto and the power and influence of the Supreme Court. The effect of establishing the supremacy of this branch of the government was to make the legal profession virtually a ruling class. To their charge was committed under our system of government the final authority in all matters of legislation. They largely represent by virtue of their training and by reason of the interests with which they are affiliated, the conservative as opposed to the democratic influences. The power and influence exerted by lawyers in this country are the natural outgrowth of the constitutional position of our Supreme Court. Its supremacy is in the last analysis the supremacy of lawyers as a class and through them of the various interests which they represent and from which they derive their support. This explains the fact so often commented on by foreign critics, that in this country lawyers exert a predominant influence in political matters.

We are still keeping alive in our legal and constitutional literature the eighteenth-century notion of liberty. Our future lawyers and judges are still trained in the old conception of government—that the chief purpose of a constitution is to limit the power of the majority. In the meantime all other democratic countries have outgrown this early conception which characterized the infancy of democracy. They have in theory at least repudiated the eighteenth-century doctrine that the few have a right to thwart the will of the many. The majority has in such countries become the only recognized source of legitimate authority. "There is no fulcrum *outside* of the majority, and therefore there is nothing on which, as *against* the majority, resistance or lengthened opposition can lean." [4] This statement was made with reference to France, but it would apply as well to England, Switzerland, and all other countries in which the principle of majority rule has received full recognition.

On the other hand American constitutional and legal literature

Emil G. Boutmy, *Studies in Constitutional Law,* English trans. (New York, 1891), p. 155.

still inculcates and keeps alive fear and distrust of majority rule. The official and ruling class in this country has been profoundly influenced by political ideas which have long been discarded in the countries which have made the most rapid strides in the direction of popular government. The influence which our constitutional and legal literature, based as it is upon a profound distrust of majority rule, has had upon the lawyers, politicians, and public men of this country can hardly be overestimated. It is true that many who have been most influenced by this spirit of distrust toward popular government would be unwilling to admit that they are opposed to majority rule—in fact, they may regard themselves as sincere believers in democracy. This is not to be wondered at when we consider that throughout our history under the Constitution the old and the new have been systematically jumbled in our political literature. In fact, the main effort of our constitutional writers would appear to be to give to the undemocratic eighteenth-century political ideas a garb and setting that would in a measure reconcile them with the democratic point of view. The natural and inevitable result has followed. The students of American political literature have imbibed the fundamental idea of the old system— its distrust of majority rule—along with a certain sentimental attachment to and acceptance of the outward forms of democracy. This irreconcilable contradiction between the form and the substance, the body and the spirit of our political institutions is not generally recognized even by the American students of government. Constitutional writers have been too much preoccupied with the thought of defending and glorifying the work of the fathers and not enough interested in disclosing its true relation to present-day thought and tendencies. As a consequence of this, the political ideas of our educated classes represent a curious admixture of democratic beliefs superimposed upon a hardly conscious substratum of eighteenth-century doctrines. It is this contradiction in our thinking that has been one of our chief sources of difficulty in dealing with political problems. While honestly believing that we have been endeavoring to make democracy a success, we have at the same time tenaciously held on to the essential features of a political system designed for the purpose of defeating the ends of popular government.

3 / A POSITIVE ROLE FOR POLICE POWER

In 1903, Oregon passed a law prohibiting the employment
of women in factories and laundries for more than ten
hours a day. A laundry owner challenged the validity of
the law and under the Constitution carried his case to
the United States Supreme Court. Louis D. Brandeis,
counsel for the state of Oregon, submitted an unusual
brief, which the Court accepted. He summarized his legal
arguments and precedents in less than a page and went
on to fill over a hundred pages with medical and
sociological data to demonstrate that the regulation of
the hours of work for women was necessary for the public
health and safety, as well as for the health and safety
of the women employees; therefore, the law was well
within the bounds of the police power of the state. By
accepting sociological, medical, and statistical evidence as
the basis of judicial decisions, the Supreme Court enlarged
the scope of the police power of the state to protect the
people from exploitation. The approach would be
important later in Brown v. *Board of Education,*
which upset the doctrine of separate but equal applied
by Plessy v. *Ferguson, without contradicting any of*
the legal reasoning in that case.

CONCLUSION

We submit that in view of the facts above set forth and of legislative action extending over a period of more than sixty years in the
leading countries of Europe, and in twenty of our States, it cannot
be said that the Legislature of Oregon had no reasonable ground
for believing that the public health, safety, or welfare did not require a legal limitation on women's work in manufacturing and

SOURCE: Muller v. Oregon, 208 U.S. 412 (1908).

mechanical establishments and laundries to ten hours in one day. See *Holden* v. *Hardy*, 169 U.S. 366, 395, 397.

Louis D. Brandeis,
Counsel for State of Oregon

Boston, *January*, 1908.

. . . . .

"(2) Because the statute does not apply equally to all persons similarly situated, and is class legislation.

"(3) The statute is not a valid exercise of the police power. The kinds of work proscribed are not unlawful, nor are they declared to be immoral or dangerous to the public health; nor can such a law be sustained on the ground that it is designed to protect women on account of their sex. There is no necessary or reasonable connection between the limitation prescribed by the act and the public health, safety or welfare."

It is the law of Oregon that women, whether married or single, have equal contractual and personal rights with men. As said by Chief Justice Wolverton, in *First National Bank* v. *Leonard*, 36 Oregon, 390, 396, after a review of the various statutes of the State upon the subject:

We may therefore say with perfect confidence that, with these three sections upon the statute book, the wife can deal, not only with her separate property, acquired from whatever source, in the same manner as her husband can with property belonging to him, but that she may make contracts and incur liabilities, and the same may be enforced against her, the same as if she were a *femme sole*. There is now no residuum of civil disability resting upon her which is not recognized as existing against the husband. The current runs steadily and strongly in the direction of the emancipation of the wife, and the policy, as disclosed by all recent legislation upon the subject in this State, is to place her upon the same footing as if she were a *femme sole*, not only with respect to her separate property, but as it affects her right to make binding contracts; and the most natural corollary to the situation is that the remedies for the enforcement of liabilities incurred are made co-extensive and co-equal with such enlarged conditions.

It thus appears that, putting to one side the elective franchise, in the matter of personal and contractual rights they stand on the same plane as the other sex. Their rights in these respects can no more be infringed than the equal rights of their brothers. We held in *Lochner* v. *New York,* 198 U.S. 45, that a law providing that no laborer shall be required or permitted to work in a bakery more than sixty hours in a week or ten hours in a day was not as to men a legitimate exercise of the police power of the State, but an unreasonable, unnecessary and arbitrary interference with the right and liberty of the individual to contract in relation to his labor, and as such was in conflict with, and void under, the Federal Constitution. That decision is invoked by plaintiff in error as decisive of the question before us. But this assumes that the difference between the sexes does not justify a different rule respecting a restriction of the hours of labor.

In patent cases counsel are apt to open the argument with a discussion of the state of the art. It may not be amiss, in the present case, before examining the constitutional question, to notice the course of legislation as well as expressions of opinion from other than judicial sources. In the brief filed by Mr. Louis D. Brandeis, for the defendant in error, is a very copious collection of all these matters, an epitome of which is found in the margin.[1]

While there have been but few decisions bearing directly upon the question, the following sustain the constitutionality of such legislation: *Commonwealth* v. *Hamilton Mfg. Co.,* 120 Massa-

---

[1] The following legislation of the States impose restrictions in some form or another upon the hours of labor that may be required of women: Massachusetts: chap. 221, 1874, Rev. Laws 1902, chap. 106, § 24; Rhode Island: 1885, Acts and Resolves 1902, chap. 994, p. 73; Louisiana: § 4, Act 43, p. 55, Laws of 1886, Rev. Laws 1904, vol. 1, p. 989; Connecticut: 1887, Gen. Stat. revision 1902, § 4691; Maine: chap. 139, 1887, Rev. Stat. 1903, chap. 40, § 48, p. 401; New Hampshire: 1887, Laws 1907, chap. 94, p. 95; Maryland: chap. 455, 1888, Pub. Gen. Laws 1903, art. 100, § 1; Virginia: p. 150, 1889-1890, Code 1904, tit. 51A, chap. 178A, § 3657*b*; Pennsylvania: No. 26, p. 30, 1897, Laws 1905, No. 226, p. 352; New York: Laws 1899, § 1, chap. 560, p. 752, Laws 1907, chap. 507, § 77, subdiv. 3, p. 1078; Nebraska: 1899, Comp. Stat. 1905, § 7955, p. 1986; Washington: Stat. 1901, chap. 68, § 1, p. 118; Colorado: Acts 1903, chap. 138, § 3, p. 310; New Jersey: 1892, Gen. Stat. 1895, p. 2350, §§ 66, 67; Oklahoma: 1890, Rev. Stat. 1903, chap. 25, art. 58, § 729; North Dakota: 1877, Rev. Code 1905, § 9440; South Dakota: 1877, Rev. Code (Penal Code, § 764), p. 1185; Wisconsin: § 1, chap. 83, Laws of 1867, Code 1898, § 1728; South Carolina: Acts 1907, No. 233, p. 487.

In foreign legislation Mr. Brandeis calls attention to these statutes: Great Britain: Factories Act of 1844, chap. 15, pp. 161, 171; Factory and Workshop

chusetts, 383; *Wenham* v. *State*, 65 Nebraska, 394, 400, 406; *State* v. *Buchanan*, 29 Washington, 602; *Commonwealth* v. *Beatty*, 15 Pa. Sup. Ct. 5, 17; against them is the case of *Ritchie* v. *People*, 155 Illinois, 98.

The legislation and opinions referred to in the margin may not be, technically speaking, authorities, and in them is little or no discussion of the constitutional question presented to us for determination, yet they are significant of a widespread belief that woman's physical structure, and the functions she performs in consequence thereof, justify special legislation restricting or qualifying the conditions under which she should be permitted to toil. Constitutional questions, it is true, are not settled by even a consensus of present public opinion, for it is the peculiar value of a written constitution that it places in unchanging form limitations upon legislative action, and thus gives a permanence and stability to popular government which otherwise would be lacking. At the same time, when a question of fact is debated and debatable, and the extent to which a special constitutional limitation goes is affected by the truth in respect to that fact, a widespread and long continued belief concerning it is worthy of consideration. We take judicial cognizance of all matters of general knowledge.

It is undoubtedly true, as more than once declared by this court,

---

Act of 1901, chap. 22, pp. 60, 71; and see 1 Edw. VII, chap. 22. France, 1848; Act Nov. 2, 1892, and March 30, 1900. Switzerland, Canton of Glarus, 1848; Federal Law 1877, art. 2, § 1. Austria, 1855; Acts 1897, art. 96*a*, §§ 1-3. Holland, 1889; art. 5, § 1. Italy, June 19, 1902, art. 7. Germany, Laws 1891.

Then follow extracts from over ninety reports of committees, bureaus of statistics, commissioners of hygiene, inspectors of factories, both in this country and in Europe, to the effect that long hours of labor are dangerous for women, primarily because of their special physical organization. The matter is discussed in these reports in different aspects, but all agree as to the danger. It would of course take too much space to give these reports in detail. Following them are extracts from similar reports discussing the general benefits of short hours from an economic aspect of the question. In many of these reports individual instances are given tending to support the general conclusion. Perhaps the general scope and character of all these reports may be summed up in what an inspector for Hanover says: "The reasons for the reduction of the working day to ten hours—(*a*) the physical organization of women, (*b*) her maternal functions, (*c*) the rearing and education of the children, (*d*) the maintenance of the home—are all so important and so far reaching that the need for such reduction need hardly be discussed."

that the general right to contract in relation to one's business is part of the liberty of the individual, protected by the Fourteenth Amendment to the Federal Constitution; yet it is equally well settled that this liberty is not absolute and extending to all contracts, and that a State may, without conflicting with the provisions of the Fourteenth Amendment, restrict in many respects the individual's power of contract. Without stopping to discuss at length the extent to which a State may act in this respect, we refer to the following cases in which the question has been considered: *Allgeyer* v. *Louisiana*, 165 U.S. 578; *Holden* v. *Hardy*, 169 U.S. 366; *Lochner* v. *New York*, 198 U.S. 45.

That woman's physical structure and the performance of maternal functions place her at a disadvantage in the struggle for subsistence is obvious. This is especially true when the burdens of motherhood are upon her. Even when they are not, by abundant testimony of the medical fraternity continuance for a long time on her feet at work, repeating this from day to day, tends to injurious effects upon the body, and as healthy mothers are essential to vigorous offspring, the physical well-being of woman becomes an object of public interest and care in order to preserve the strength and vigor of the race.

Still again, history discloses the fact that woman has always been dependent upon man. He established his control at the outset by superior physical strength, and this control in various forms, with diminishing intensity, has continued to the present. As a minor, though not to the same extent, she has been looked upon in the courts as needing especial care that her rights may be preserved. Education was long denied her, and while now the doors of the school room are opened and her opportunities for acquiring knowledge are great, yet even with that and the consequent increase of capacity for business affairs it is still true that in the struggle for subsistence she is not an equal competitor with her brother. Though limitations upon personal and contractual rights may be removed by legislation, there is that in her disposition and habits of life which will operate against a full assertion of those rights. She will still be where some legislation to protect her seems necessary to secure a real equality of right. Doubtless there are individual exceptions, and there are many respects in which she has an advantage over him; but looking at it from the viewpoint of the effort to maintain an independent position in life, she is not upon an equality. Differentiated by these matters from the other sex, she is properly placed in a class by herself, and legislation designed for her protection may be sustained, even when like legislation is not necessary for men and could not be sustained. It is impossible to close one's eyes to the fact that she still looks to her brother and depends upon him. Even though all restrictions on political, personal and contractual rights were taken away, and she stood, so far as statutes are concerned, upon an absolutely equal plane with him, it would still be true that she is so constituted that she will rest upon and look to him for protection; that her physical structure and a proper discharge of her maternal functions—having in view not merely her own health, but the well-being of the race—justify legislation to protect her from the greed as well as the passion of man. The limitations which this statute places upon her contractual powers, upon her right to agree with her employer as to the time she shall labor, are not imposed solely for her benefit, but also largely for the benefit of all. Many words cannot make this plainer. The two sexes differ in structure of body, in the functions to be performed by each, in the amount of physical strength, in the capacity for long-continued labor, particularly when done standing, in the influence of vigorous health upon the future well-being of the race, in the self-reliance which enables one to assert full rights, and in the capacity to maintain the struggle for subsistence. This difference justifies a difference in legislation and upholds that which is designed to compensate for some of the burdens which rest upon her.

We have not referred in this discussion to the denial of the elective franchise in the State of Oregon, for while it may disclose a lack of political equality in all things with her brother, that is not of itself decisive. The reason runs deeper, and rests in the inherent difference between the two sexes, and in the different functions in life which they perform.

For these reasons, and without questioning in any respect the decision in *Lochner* v. *New York,* we are of the opinion that it cannot be adjudged that the act in question is in conflict with the Federal Constitution, so far as it respects the work of a female in a laundry, and the judgment of the Supreme Court of Oregon is

Affirmed.

4 / A NEW ROLE FOR GOVERNMENT: THE NEW NATIONALISM

*Herbert David Croly was born in New York City in 1869
and grew up in a journalistic atmosphere. His father,
David Goodman Croly, was an editor of the New York*
World *and later of the* Daily Graphic, *and was also a
pioneer in the birth control movement. His mother, Jane
Cunningham Croly, was one of America's most prominent
women journalists and a leader in the equal rights
movement. Herbert had a sporadic college career at
Harvard, finally obtaining his bachelor's degree in 1910.
Meanwhile, between 1900 and 1906 he edited the*
Architectural Record, *but then stepped down from the
post, although not from the staff, in order to write his
first and most influential book,* The Promise of American
Life. *In 1914, along with Walter Weyl and Walter
Lippmann, he founded* The New Republic, *one of the
most important journals of opinion in the United States.
Theodore Roosevelt read Croly's book enthusiastically.
Croly gave Roosevelt no new ideas but helped crystallize
his thinking and provided him with the catch-phrase
"New Nationalism." Croly insisted that under the new
industrial conditions, Hamiltonian means—a strong
central government—were needed to obtain Jeffersonian
ends—freedom and democracy. He proposed to harness
nationalism to serve the general welfare. In his enthusiasm
he ignored the possibility that nationalism might also
be used to support totalitarianism and the denial of the
freedom that he sought.*

SOURCE: Herbert Croly, *The Promise of American Life* (New York: The Macmillan Company, 1909), pp. 148-54.

II. The Logic of Reform

The prevailing preconception of the reformers, that the existing evils and abuses have been due chiefly to the energy and lack of scruple with which business men and politicians have taken advantage of the good but easy-going American, and that a general increase of moral energy, assisted by some minor legal changes, will restore the balance,—such a conception of the situation is less than half true. No doubt, the "plain people" of the United States have been morally indifferent, and have allowed unscrupulous special interests to usurp too much power; but that is far from being the whole story. The unscrupulous energy of the "Boss" or the "tainted" millionaire is vitally related to the moral indifference of the "plain people." Both of them have been encouraged to believe by the nature of our traditional ideas and institutions that a man could be patriotic without being either public-spirited or disinterested. The democratic state has been conceived as a piece of political machinery, which existed for the purpose of securing certain individual rights and opportunities—the expectation being that the greatest individual happiness would be thereby promoted, and one which harmonized with the public interest. Consequently when the "Boss" and the "tainted" millionaire took advantage of this situation to secure for themselves an unusually large amount of political and economic power, they were putting into practice an idea which traditionally had been entirely respectable, and which during the pioneer period had not worked badly. On the other hand, when the mass of American voters failed to detect the danger of such usurpation until it had gone altogether too far, they, too, were not without warrant for their lethargy and callousness. They, too, in a smaller way had considered the American political and economic system chiefly as a system framed for their individual benefit, and it did not seem sportsmanlike to turn and rend their more successful competitors, until they were told that the "trusts" and the "Bosses" were violating the sacred principle of equal rights. Thus the abuses of which we are complaining are not weeds which have been allowed to spring up from neglect, and which can be eradicated by a man with a hoe. They are cultivated plants, which, if not precisely specified in the plan of the American political and economic garden, have at least been encouraged by traditional methods of cultivation.

The fact that this dangerous usurpation of power has been accomplished partly by illegal methods has blinded many reformers to two considerations, which have a vital relation to both the theory and the practice of reform. Violation of the law was itself partly the result of conflicting and unwise state legislation, and for this reason did not seem very heinous either to its perpetrators or to public opinion. But even if the law had not been violated, similar results would have followed. Under the traditional American system, with the freedom permitted to the individual, with the restriction placed on the central authority, and with its assumption of a substantial identity between the individual and the public interest—under such a system unusually energetic and unscrupulous men were bound to seize a kind and an amount of political and economic power which was not entirely wholesome. They had a license to do so; and if they had failed to take advantage thereof, their failure would have been an indication, not of disinterestedness or moral impeccability, but of sheer weakness and inefficiency.

How utterly confusing it is, consequently, to consider reform as equivalent merely to the restoration of the American democracy to a former condition of purity and excellence! Our earlier political and economic condition was not at its best a fit subject for any great amount of complacency. It cannot be restored, even if we would; and the public interest has nothing to gain by its restoration. The usurpation of power by "trusts" and "Bosses" is more than anything else an expression of a desirable individual initiative and organizing ability—which have been allowed to become dangerous and partly corrupt, because of the incoherence and the lack of purpose and responsibility in the traditional American political and economic system. A "purification" might well destroy the good with the evil; and even if it were successful in eradicating certain abuses, would only prepare the way for the outbreak in another form of the tendency towards individual aggrandizement and social classification. No amount of moral energy, directed merely towards the enforcement of the laws, can possibly avail to accomplish any genuine or lasting reform. It is the laws themselves which are partly at fault, and still more at fault is the group of ideas and traditional practices behind the laws.

Reformers have failed for the most part to reach a correct diagnosis of existing political and economic abuses, because they are almost as much the victim of perverted, confused, and routine habits of political thought as is the ordinary politician. They have eschewed the tradition of partisan conformity in reference to controverted political questions, but they have not eschewed a still more insidious tradition of conformity—the tradition that a patriotic American citizen must not in his political thinking go beyond the formulas consecrated in the sacred American writings. They adhere to the stupefying rule that the good Fathers of the Republic relieved their children from the necessity of vigorous, independent, or consistent thinking in political matters,—that it is the duty of their loyal children to repeat the sacred words and then await a miraculous consummation of individual and social prosperity. Accordingly, all the leading reformers begin by piously reiterating certain phrases about equal rights for all and special privileges for none, and of government of the people, by the people, and for the people. Having in this way proved their fundamental political orthodoxy, they proceed to interpret the phrases according to their personal, class, local, and partisan preconceptions and interests. They have never stopped to inquire whether the principle of equal rights in its actual embodiment in American institutional and political practice has not been partly responsible for some of the existing abuses, whether it is either a safe or sufficient platform for a reforming movement, and whether its continued proclamation as the fundamental political principle of a democracy will help or hinder the higher democratic consummation. Their unquestioning orthodoxy in this respect has made them faithless both to their own personal interest as reformers and to the cause of reform. Reform exclusively as a moral protest and awakening is condemned to sterility. Reformers exclusively as moral protestants and purifiers are condemned to misdirected effort, to an illiberal puritanism, and to personal self-stultification. Reform must necessarily mean an intellectual as well as a moral challenge; and its higher purposes will never be accomplished unless it is accompanied by a masterful and jubilant intellectual awakening.

All Americans, whether they are professional politicians or reformers, "predatory" millionaires or common people, political philosophers or schoolboys, accept the principle of "equal rights for all and special privileges for none" as the absolutely sufficient rule of an American democratic political system. The platforms of both parties testify on its behalf. Corporation lawyers and their clients appear frequently to believe in it. Tammany offers tribute to it during every local political campaign in New York. A Democratic Senator, in the intervals between his votes for increased duties on the products of his state, declares it to be the summary of all political wisdom. The fact that Mr. Bryan incorporates it in most of his speeches does not prevent Mr. Hearst from keeping it standing in type for the purpose of showing how very American the *American* can be. The fact that Mr. Hearst has appropriated it with the American flag as belonging peculiarly to himself has not prevented Mr. Roosevelt from explaining the whole of his policy of reform as at bottom an attempt to restore a "Square Deal"—that is, a condition of equal rights and non-existing privileges. More radical reformers find the same principle equally useful for their own purposes. Mr. Frederic C. Howe, in his "Hope of Democracy," bases an elaborate scheme of municipal socialism exclusively upon it. Mr. William Smythe, in his "Constructive Democracy," finds warrant in the same principle for the immediate purchase by the central government of the railway and "trust" franchises. Mr. Henry George, Jr., in his "Menace of Privilege," asserts that the plain American citizen can never enjoy equality of rights as long as land, mines, railroad rights of way and terminals, and the like remain in the hands of private owners. The collectivist socialists are no less certain that the institution of private property necessarily gives some men an unjust advantage over others. There is no extreme of radicalism or conservatism, of individualism or socialism, of Republicanism or Democracy, which does not rest its argument on this one consummate principle.

In this respect the good American finds himself in a situation similar to that with which he was confronted before the Civil War. At that time, also, Abolitionist and slave-holder, Republican and pioneer Democrat, each of them declared himself to be the interpreter of the true democratic doctrine; and no substantial progress could be made towards the settlement of the question, until public opinion had been instructed as to the real meaning of democracy in relation to the double-headed problem of slavery and states' rights. It required the utmost intellectual courage and ability to emancipate the conception of democracy from the illusions and confusions of thought which enabled Davis, Douglas, and Garrison all to pose as impeccable democrats; and at the present time reformers need to devote as much ability and more courage to the task of framing a fitting creed for a reformed and reforming American democracy.

The political lessons of the anti-slavery and states' rights discussions may not be of much obvious assistance in thinking out such a creed; but they should at least help the reformers to understand the methods whereby the purposes of a reformed democracy can be achieved. No progress was made towards the solution of the slavery question until the question itself was admitted to be national in scope, and its solution a national responsibility. No substantial progress had been made in the direction of reform until it began to be understood that here, also, a national responsibility existed, which demanded an exercise of the powers of the central government. Reform is both meaningless and powerless unless the Jeffersonian principle of non-interference is abandoned. The experience of the last generation plainly shows that the American economic and social system cannot be allowed to take care of itself, and that the automatic harmony of the individual and the public interest, which is the essence of the Jeffersonian democratic creed, has proved to be an illusion. Interference with the natural course of individual and popular action there must be in the public interest; and such interference must at least be sufficient to accomplish its purposes. The house of the American democracy is again by way of being divided against itself, because the national interest has not been consistently asserted as against special and local interests; and again, also, it can be reunited only by being partly reconstructed on better foundations. If reform does not and cannot mean restoration, it is bound to mean reconstruction.

The reformers have come partly to realize that the Jeffersonian policy of drift must be abandoned. They no longer expect the American ship of state by virtue of its own righteous framework to sail away to a safe harbor in the Promised Land. They understand that there must be a vigorous and conscious assertion of the public as opposed to private and special interests, and that the American people must to a greater extent than they have in the past subordinate the latter to the former. They behave as if the American ship of state will hereafter require careful steering; and a turn or two at the wheel has given them some idea of the course they must set. On the other hand, even the best of them have not learned the name of its ultimate destination, the full difficulties of the navigation, or the stern discipline which may eventually be imposed upon the ship's crew. They do not realize, that is, how thoroughly Jeffersonian individualism must be abandoned for the benefit of a genuinely individual and social consummation; and they do not realize how dangerous and fallacious a chart their cherished principle of equal rights may well become. In reviving the practice of vigorous national action for the achievement of a national purpose, the better reformers have, if they only knew it, been looking in the direction of a much more trustworthy and serviceable political principle. The assumption of such a responsibility implies the rejection of a large part of the Jeffersonian creed, and a renewed attempt to establish in its place the popularity of its Hamiltonian rival. On the other hand, it involves no less surely the transformation of Hamiltonianism into a thoroughly democratic political principle. None of these inferences have, however, as yet been generally drawn, and no leading reformer has sought to give reform its necessary foundation of positive political principle.

Only a very innocent person will expect reformers to be convinced of such a novel notion of reform by mere assertion, no matter how emphatic, or by argument, no matter how conclusive. But if, as I have said, reform actually implies a criticism of traditional American ideas, and a more responsible and more positive conception of democracy, these implications will necessarily be revealed in the future history of the reforming agitation. The reformers who understand will be assisted by the logic of events, whereas those who cannot and will not understand will be thwarted by the logic of events. Gradually (it may be anticipated) reformers who dare to criticise and who are not afraid to reconstruct will be sharply distinguished from reformers who believe reform to be a species of higher conservatism. The latter will be forced where they belong into the ranks of the supporters and beneficiaries of the existing system; and the party of genuine reform will be strengthened by their departure. On the other hand, the sincere and thorough-going reformers can hardly avoid a division into two divergent groups. One of these groups will stick faithfully to the principle of equal rights and to the spirit of the true Jeffersonian faith. It will seek still further to undermine the representative character of American institutions, to deprive official leadership of any genuine responsibility, and to cultivate individualism at the expense of individual and national integrity. The second group, on the other hand, may learn from experience that the principle of equal rights is a dangerous weapon in the hands of factious and merely revolutionary agitators, and even that such a principle is only a partial and poverty-stricken statement of the purpose of a democratic polity. The logic of its purposes will compel it to favor the principle of responsible representative government, and it will seek to forge institutions which will endow responsible political government with renewed life. Above all, it may discover that the attempt to unite the Hamiltonian principle of national political responsibility and efficiency with a frank democratic purpose will give a new meaning to the Hamiltonian system of political ideas and a new power to democracy.

5 / A NEW ROLE FOR GOVERNMENT: THE NEW FREEDOM

Louis D. Brandeis was born in Louisville, Kentucky, in 1856. He attended the University of Louisville and obtained his law degree from Harvard in 1877. He was admitted to the bar in St. Louis in 1878 and practiced in Boston from 1879 to 1916, when he was appointed Associate Justice of the Supreme Court of the

SOURCE: *The Curse of Bigness: Miscellaneous Papers of Louis D. Brandeis*, pp. 104-8. Edited by Osmond K. Fraenkel, as projected by Clarence M. Lewis. Copyright 1934 by Louis D. Brandeis, © 1962 by Susan Brandeis Gilbert and Elizabeth Brandeis Raushenbush. Reprinted by permission of The Viking Press, Inc.

*United States. ¶Brandeis began his career
as a brilliant corporation lawyer, but
began to think seriously about social problems
during the 1894 Pullman strike. By 1900 he was deeply
involved in exposing insurance fraud and in attempts
to get regulatory legislation. It was this second career as
"the people's advocate" that embroiled him in politics and
eventually elevated him to the Supreme Court bench.
Woodrow Wilson's presidential campaign of 1912 lacked
spark and drive until Brandeis helped to focus the
emphasis on the responsibility of government to establish
the conditions of free competition. The New Freedom,
he argued, would be that of free competition, protected
from the strictures of monopoly and big business by a
strong central government.*

SHALL WE ABANDON THE POLICY OF COMPETITION?

Shall we abandon as obsolete the long-cherished policy of competition, and accept in its place the long-detested policy of monopoly? The issue is not (as it is usually stated by advocates of monopoly), "Shall we have unrestricted competition or regulated monopoly?" It is, "Shall we have regulated competition or regulated monopoly?"

Regulation is essential to the preservation and development of competition, just as it is necessary to the preservation and best development of liberty. We have long curbed physically the strong, to protect those physically weaker. More recently we have extended such prohibitions to business. We have restricted theoretical freedom of contract by factory laws. The liberty of the merchant and manufacturer to lie in trade, expressed in the fine phrase of *caveat emptor*, is yielding to the better conceptions of business ethics, before pure-food laws and postal-fraud prosecutions. Similarly, the right to competition must be limited in order to preserve it. For excesses of competition lead to monopoly, as excesses of liberty lead to absolutism. The extremes meet.

The issue, therefore, is: Regulated competition *versus* regulated monopoly. The policy of regulated competition is distinctly a constructive policy. It is the policy of development as distinguished from the destructive policy of private monopoly.

It is asserted that to persist in the disintegration of existing unlawful trusts is to pursue a policy of destruction. No statement could be more misleading. Progress demands that we remove the obstacles in the path of progress; and private monopoly is the most serious obstacle.

One has heard of late the phrases: "You can't make people compete by law." "Artificial competition is undesirable."

These are truisms, but their implication is false. The suggestion is not that traders be compelled to compete, but that they be prevented from killing competition. Equally misleading is the phrase, "Natural monopolies should not be interfered with." There are no natural monopolies today in the industrial world. The Oil Trust and the Steel Trust have been referred to as natural monopolies, but they are both most unnatural. The Oil Trust acquired its control of the market by conduct which involved flagrant violations of law. Without the aid of criminal rebating, of bribery and corruption, the Standard Oil Trust would never have acquired the vast wealth and power which enabled it to destroy its small competitors by price-cutting and similar practices.

The Steel Trust acquired control not through greater efficiency, but by buying up existing plants and ore supplies at fabulous prices. It is believed that not a single industrial monopoly exists today which is the result of natural growth. Competition has been suppressed either by ruthless practices or by an improper use of inordinate wealth and power. If the law prohibiting such practices is clearly defined and enforced, as it is the purpose of the La Follette Bill to accomplish, no similar trust will arise in the future.

The only argument that has been seriously advanced in favor of private monopoly is that competition involves waste, while the monopoly prevents waste and leads to efficiency. This argument is essentially unsound. The wastes of competition are negligible. The economies of monopoly are superficial and delusive. The efficiency of monopoly is at the best temporary.

Undoubtedly competition involves waste. What human activity does not? The wastes of democracy are among the greatest obvious wastes, but we have compensations in democracy which far outweigh that waste and make it more efficient than absolutism. So it is with competition. The waste is relatively insignificant. There are wastes of competition which do not develop, but kill. These the law can and should eliminate, by regulating competition.

It is true that the unit in business may be too small to be efficient. It is also true that the unit may be too large to be efficient, and this is no uncommon incident of monopoly.

Whenever trusts have developed efficiency, their fruits have been absorbed almost wholly by the trusts themselves. From such efficiency as they have developed, the community has gained substantially nothing.

The proposed Government commission to fix prices would not greatly relieve the evils attendant upon monopoly. It might reduce a trust's profits, but it would fail materially to reduce the trust's prices; because the limitation of the monopoly's profits would, by lessening this incentive, surely reduce the monopoly's efficiency.

To secure successful management of any private business, reward must be proportionate to success. The establishment of any rule fixing a maximum return on capital would, by placing a limit upon the fruits of achievement, tend to lessen efficiency.

No selling price for monopoly products could be set constitutionally at a point lower than that which would allow a reasonable return on capital. And in the absence of comparative data from any competing businesses producing the same article at less cost, it would be virtually impossible to determine that the cost should be lower.

The success of the Interstate Commerce Commission has been invoked as an argument in favor of licensing and regulating monopoly.

But the Interstate Commerce Commission has been effective principally in preventing rate increases and in stopping discrimination. In those instances where the Commission has reduced rates (as distinguished from preventing increases) the Commission rested its decisions largely on the ground that existing rates amounted to discriminations against particular places or articles, or the lower rates were justified by a comparison with other rates of the same or other companies. Price-fixing of that nature applied to industrial trusts would afford little protection to the public.

In the second place, there is a radical difference between attempts to fix rates for transportation and similar public services, and fixing prices in industrial businesses. Problems of transportation, while varying infinitely in detail, are largely the same throughout the whole country, and they are largely the same yesterday, today, and tomorrow. In industry we have, instead of uniformity, infinite variety; instead of stability, constant change.

In the third place, the problems of the Interstate Commerce Commission, relatively simple as they are, already far exceed the capacity of that or any single board. Think of the infinite questions which would come before an industrial commission seeking to fix rates, and the suffering of the community from the inability of that body promptly and efficiently to dispose of them.

Every business requires for its business health the *memento mori* of competition from without. It requires likewise a certain competition from within, which can exist only where the ownership and management, on the one hand, and the employees, on the other, shall each be alert, hopeful, self-respecting, and free to work out for themselves the best conceivable conditions.

The successful, the powerful trusts, have created conditions absolutely inconsistent with these—America's—industrial and social needs. It may be true that as a legal proposition mere size is not a crime, but mere size may become an industrial and social menace, because it frequently creates as against possible competitors and as against the employees conditions of such gross inequality, as to imperil the welfare of the employees and of the industry.

In the midst of our indignation over the unpardonable crimes of trade-union leaders, disclosed at Los Angeles, would not our statesmen and thinkers seek to ascertain the underlying cause of this widespread, deliberate outburst of crimes of violence? What was it that led men like the McNamaras to believe really that the only recourse they had for improving the condition of the wage-earner was to use dynamite against property and life?

Certainly it was not individual depravity. Was it not because they, and men like them, believed that the wage-earner, acting singly, or collectively, is not strong enough to secure substantial justice? Is there not a causal connection between the development of these huge indomitable trusts and the horrible crimes now under investigation? Are not these irresistible trusts important contributing causes of these crimes—these unintelligent expressions of despairing social unrest? Is it not irony to speak of the equality of opportunity, in a country cursed with their bigness?

The right of labor to organize and to deal collectively with its employers should not be curtailed.

There is not the slightest danger that labor will assume control of industry. It has become exceedingly difficult for the unions to maintain themselves because of the constant inflow of foreign labor and the great number of non-union men. This maintains a state of competition, which, did it exist in the industrial and financial business of the country, would make unnecessary any change in existing laws.

The only right claimed by the labor unions is that of collective bargaining, and this right employers also should have and exercise. It would be perfectly proper for independent competing employers to form employers' organizations, and to deal with the labor unions upon exactly the same footing as is the case with unions—that is, collectively.

Nothing has been done to improve the conditions under which men labor, that has not increased their efficiency. Shorter hours often lead to greater production; and there is economy in high wages.

PART II

The Quest for Cultural Freedom

(1920-1929)

B$_Y$ 1920 the Progressive battle for freedom from the shackles of economic individualism and strict constructionism was largely won. However, the activities and achievements of the social reformers and the "gas and water socialists" tended to obscure the faint rumblings of cultural revolution emanating from little magazines, little theaters, artists' colonies, and off-beat gatherings in Mabel Dodge's apartment on New York's Fifth Avenue or Stieglitz's attic gallery. Following the First World War, the widespread disillusionment that paralyzed the social reform movement galvanized a cultural rebellion in which the rebels fought for freedom from the stultifying restrictions of the puritan moral and literary standards of the Victorian era and against the materialism and dominance of the machine of industrial capitalism (Selection 6). Writers, artists, dramatists, and poets of the 1920's, unlike the Progressives, were passionately concerned with the individual, not society, with private, not public experience. Their fight was for recognition of the right of creative individuals to free expression (Selections 7, 8, 9).

The decade of the twenties is often characterized as a destructive era, an era of cults, art for art's sake, and poetry for poets only. It was a time when H. L. Mencken, arising to belated fame, ridiculed all the cherished values of the American "booboisie," and Lewis Mumford denounced assembly-line mechanization as destructive of man's humanity. The period was certainly rife with a literature of self-deprecation; nevertheless, at the very time when intellectuals were claiming that art could not flourish in America, painting, drama, poetry, and literature blossomed as never before. The negativism of the critics, the sneering satire of F. Scott Fitzgerald, or nihilistic naturalism of Joseph Wood Krutch (Selection 10), both of whom had "grown up to find all gods dead, all wars fought, all faith in man shaken," were not symptoms of despair but of the agony of change. Playwrights like Eugene O'Neill and Maxwell Anderson emerged from stable theaters to revolutionize American drama. Hart Crane, E. E. Cummings, Conrad Aiken, Marianne Moore, and Wallace Stevens rejuvenated American poetry, and the novels of Ernest Hemingway, William Faulkner, Sherwood Anderson, Willa Cather, F. Scott Fitzgerald, and Sinclair Lewis testify to the creativity of the period. The rejection and systematic demolition of formal tradition and naive idealism brought cultural freedom and cleared the way for one of the most creative periods in the history of the arts in America.

6 / THE REVOLT AGAINST FORMALISM IN PHILOSOPHY

George Santayana was born in Madrid, Spain, in 1863, but grew up in the United States. After graduating from Harvard in 1886, he studied at the University of Berlin. In 1889 he returned to serve on the Harvard faculty, teaching philosophy until his resignation in 1911 when he went to Europe again, this time to live and write until his death in 1952. Santayana was the greatest American philosopher of naturalism and opponent of philosophic idealism. He expressed his ideas at length in the monumental study The Life of Reason, or the Faces of Human Progress *(5 vols., 1905-1906). The following selection, "The Genteel Tradition in American Philosophy," gave a name to the pattern of ideas and attitudes against*

SOURCE: George Santayana, *The Winds of Doctrine* (London: J. M. Dent & Sons Ltd., 1913), pp. 186-215.

which the artists and writers of the 1920's revolted.
This essay is a study of the entire philosophical tradition
in America, and is one of the most incisive and famous
criticisms of transcendentalism and idealism in
American philosophy.

Address delivered before the Philosophical Union of the University
of California, August 25, 1911.

LADIES AND GENTLEMEN,—The privilege of addressing you to-day
is very welcome to me, not merely for the honour of it, which is
great, nor for the pleasures of travel, which are many, when it is
California that one is visiting for the first time, but also because
there is something I have long wanted to say which this occasion
seems particularly favourable for saying. America is still a young
country, and this part of it is especially so; and it would have been
nothing extraordinary if, in this young country, material preoccupations had altogether absorbed people's minds, and they had been
too much engrossed in living to reflect upon life, or to have any
philosophy. The opposite, however, is the case. Not only have you
already found time to philosophise in California, as your society
proves, but the eastern colonists from the very beginning were a
sophisticated race. As much as in clearing the land and fighting the
Indians they were occupied, as they expressed it, in wrestling with
the Lord. The country was new, but the race was tried, chastened,
and full of solemn memories. It was an old wine in new bottles;
and America did not have to wait for its present universities, with
their departments of academic philosophy, in order to possess a
living philosophy—to have a distinct vision of the universe and
definite convictions about human destiny.

Now this situation is a singular and remarkable one, and has
many consequences, not all of which are equally fortunate. America
is a young country with an old mentality: it has enjoyed the advantages of a child carefully brought up and thoroughly indoc-
trinated; it has been a wise child. But a wise child, an old head on
young shoulders, always has a comic and an unpromising side.
The wisdom is a little thin and verbal, not aware of its full meaning
and grounds; and physical and emotional growth may be stunted
by it, or even deranged. Or when the child is too vigorous for that,

he will develop a fresh mentality of his own, out of his observations and actual instincts; and this fresh mentality will interfere with the traditional mentality, and tend to reduce it to something perfunctory, conventional, and perhaps secretly despised. A philosophy is not genuine unless it inspires and expresses the life of those who cherish it. I do not think the hereditary philosophy of America has done much to atrophy the natural activities of the inhabitants; the wise child has not missed the joys of youth or of manhood; but what has happened is that the hereditary philosophy has grown stale, and that the academic philosophy afterwards developed has caught the stale odour from it. America is not simply, as I said a moment ago, a young country with an old mentality: it is a country with two mentalities, one a survival of the beliefs and standards of the fathers, the other an expression of the instincts, practice, and discoveries of the younger generations. In all the higher things of the mind—in religion, in literature, in the moral emotions—it is the hereditary spirit that still prevails, so much so that Mr. Bernard Shaw finds that America is a hundred years behind the times. The truth is that one-half of the American mind, that not occupied intensely in practical affairs, has remained, I will not say high-and-dry, but slightly becalmed; it has floated gently in the back-water, while, alongside, in invention and industry and social organisation, the other half of the mind was leaping down a sort of Niagara Rapids. This division may be found symbolised in American architecture: a neat reproduction of the colonial mansion—with some modern comforts introduced surreptitiously—stands beside the sky-scraper. The American Will inhabits the sky-scraper; the American Intellect inhabits the colonial mansion. The one is the sphere of the American man; the other, at least predominantly, of the American woman. The one is all aggressive enterprise; the other is all genteel tradition.

Now, with your permission, I should like to analyse more fully how this interesting situation has arisen, how it is qualified, and whither it tends. And in the first place we should remember what, precisely, that philosophy was which the first settlers brought with them into the country. In strictness there was more than one; but we may confine our attention to what I will call Calvinism, since it is on this that the current academic philosophy has been grafted. I do not mean exactly the Calvinism of Calvin, or even of Jonathan

Edwards; for in their systems there was much that was not pure philosophy, but rather faith in the externals and history of revelation. Jewish and Christian revelation was interpreted by these men, however, in the spirit of a particular philosophy, which might have arisen under any sky, and been associated with any other religion as well as with Protestant Christianity. In fact, the philosophical principle of Calvinism appears also in the Koran, in Spinoza, and in Cardinal Newman; and persons with no very distinctive Christian belief, like Carlyle or like Professor [Josiah] Royce, may be nevertheless, philosophically, perfect Calvinists. Calvinism, taken in this sense, is an expression of the agonised conscience. It is a view of the world which an agonised conscience readily embraces, if it takes itself seriously, as, being agonised, of course it must. Calvinism, essentially, asserts three things: that sin exists, that sin is punished, and that it is beautiful that sin should exist to be punished. The heart of the Calvinist is therefore divided between tragic concern at his own miserable condition, and tragic exultation about the universe at large. He oscillates between a profound abasement and a paradoxical elation of the spirit. To be a Calvinist philosophically is to feel a fierce pleasure in the existence of misery, especially of one's own, in that this misery seems to manifest the fact that the Absolute is irresponsible or infinite or holy. Human nature, it feels, is totally depraved: to have the instincts and motives that we necessarily have is a great scandal, and we must suffer for it; but that scandal is requisite, since otherwise the serious importance of being as we ought to be would not have been vindicated.

To those of us who have not an agonised conscience this system may seem fantastic and even unintelligible; yet it is logically and intently thought out from its emotional premises. It can take permanent possession of a deep mind here and there, and under certain conditions it can become epidemic. Imagine, for instance, a small nation with an intense vitality, but on the verge of ruin, ecstatic and distressful, having a strict and minute code of laws, that paints life in sharp and violent chiaroscuro, all pure righteousness and black abominations, and exaggerating the consequences of both perhaps to infinity. Such a people were the Jews after the exile, and again the early Protestants. If such a people is philosophical at all, it will not improbably be Calvinistic. Even in the early American communities many of these conditions were fulfilled. The nation was small and isolated; it lived under pressure and constant trial; it was acquainted with but a small range of goods and evils. Vigilance over conduct and an absolute demand for personal integrity were not merely traditional things, but things that practical sages, like Franklin and Washington, recommended to their countrymen, because they were virtues that justified themselves visibly by their fruits. But soon these happy results themselves helped to relax the pressure of external circumstances, and indirectly the pressure of the agonised conscience within. The nation became numerous; it ceased to be either ecstatic or distressful; the high social morality which on the whole it preserved took another colour; people remained honest and helpful out of good sense and good will rather than out of scrupulous adherence to any fixed principles. They retained their instinct for order, and often created order with surprising quickness; but the sanctity of law, to be obeyed for its own sake, began to escape them; it seemed too unpractical a notion, and not quite serious. In fact, the second and native-born American mentality began to take shape. The sense of sin totally evaporated. Nature, in the words of Emerson, was all beauty and commodity; and while operating on it laboriously, and drawing quick returns, the American began to drink in inspiration from it æsthetically. At the same time, in so broad a continent, he had elbow-room. His neighbours helped more than they hindered him; he wished their number to increase. Good will became the great American virtue; and a passion arose for counting heads, and square miles, and cubic feet, and minutes saved—as if there had been anything to save them for. How strange to the American now that saying of Jonathan Edwards, that men are naturally God's enemies! Yet that is an axiom to any intelligent Calvinist, though the words he uses may be different. If you told the modern American that he is totally depraved, he would think you were joking, as he himself usually is. He is convinced that he always has been, and always will be, victorious and blameless.

Calvinism thus lost its basis in American life. Some emotional natures, indeed, reverted in their religious revivals or private searchings of heart to the sources of the tradition; for any of the radical points of view in philosophy may cease to be prevalent, but none can cease to be possible. Other natures, more sensitive to the moral and literary influences of the world, preferred to abandon parts of their philosophy, hoping thus to reduce the distance which should separate the remainder from real life.

Meantime, if anybody arose with a special sensibility or a technical genius, he was in great straits; not being fed sufficiently by the world, he was driven in upon his own resources. The three American writers whose personal endowment was perhaps the finest —Poe, Hawthorne, and Emerson—had all a certain starved and abstract quality. They could not retail the genteel tradition; they were too keen, too perceptive, and too independent for that. But life offered them little digestible material, nor were they naturally voracious. They were fastidious, and under the circumstances they were starved. Emerson, to be sure, fed on books. There was a great catholicity in his reading; and he showed a fine tact in his comments, and in his way of appropriating what he read. But he read transcendentally, not historically, to learn what he himself felt, not what others might have felt before him. And to feed on books, for a philosopher or a poet, is still to starve. Books can help him to acquire form, or to avoid pitfalls; they cannot supply him with substance, if he is to have any. Therefore the genius of Poe and Hawthorne, and even of Emerson, was employed on a sort of inner play, or digestion of vacancy. It was a refined labour, but it was in danger of being morbid, or tinkling, or self-indulgent. It was a play of intra-mental rhymes. Their mind was like an old music-box, full of tender echoes and quaint fancies. These fancies expressed their personal genius sincerely, as dreams may; but they were arbitrary fancies in comparison with what a real observer would have said in the premises. Their manner, in a word, was subjective. In their own persons they escaped the mediocrity of the genteel tradition, but they supplied nothing to supplant it in other minds.

The churches, likewise, although they modified their spirit, had no philosophy to offer save a new emphasis on parts of what Calvinism contained. The theology of Calvin, we must remember, had much in it besides philosophical Calvinism. A Christian tenderness, and a hope of grace for the individual, came to mitigate its sardonic optimism; and it was these evangelical elements that the Calvinistic churches now emphasised, seldom and with blushes referring to hell-fire or infant damnation. Yet philosophic Calvinism, with a theory of life that would perfectly justify hell-fire and infant damnation if they happened to exist, still dominates the traditional metaphysics. It is an ingredient, and the decisive ingredient, in what calls itself idealism. But in order to see just what part Calvinism plays in current idealism, it will be necessary to distinguish the other chief element in that complex system, namely, transcendentalism.

Transcendentalism is the philosophy which the romantic era produced in Germany, and independently, I believe, in America also. Transcendentalism proper, like romanticism, is not any particular set of dogmas about what things exist; it is not a system of the universe regarded as a fact, or as a collection of facts. It is a method, a point of view, from which any world, no matter what it might contain, could be approached by a self-conscious observer. Transcendentalism is systematic subjectivism. It studies the perspectives of knowledge as they radiate from the self; it is a plan of those avenues of inference by which our ideas of things must be reached, if they are to afford any systematic or distant vistas. In other words, transcendentalism is the critical logic of science. Knowledge, it says, has a station, as in a watch-tower; it is always seated here and now, in the self of the moment. The past and the future, things inferred and things conceived, lie around it, painted as upon a panorama. They cannot be lighted up save by some centrifugal ray of attention and present interest, by some active operation of the mind.

This is hardly the occasion for developing or explaining this delicate insight; suffice it to say, lest you should think later that I disparage transcendentalism, that as a method I regard it as correct and, when once suggested, unforgettable. I regard it as the chief contribution made in modern times to speculation. But it is a method only, an attitude we may always assume if we like and that will always be legitimate. It is no answer, and involves no particular answer, to the question: What exists; in what order is what exists produced; what is to exist in the future? This question must be answered by observing the object, and tracing humbly the movement of the object. It cannot be answered at all by harping on the fact that this object, if discovered, must be discovered by somebody, and by somebody who has an interest in discovering it. Yet the Germans who first gained the full transcendental insight were romantic people; they were more or less frankly poets; they were colossal egotists, and wished to make not only their own knowledge but the whole universe centre about themselves. And full as they were of their romantic isolation and romantic liberty, it occurred to them to imagine that all reality might be a transcendental self and a romantic dreamer like themselves; nay, that it might be just their own transcendental self and their own romantic dreams extended indefinitely. Transcendental logic, the method of discovery for the mind, was to become also the method of evolution in nature and history. Transcendental method, so abused, produced transcendental myth. A conscientious critique of knowledge was turned into a sham system of nature. We must therefore distinguish sharply the transcendental grammar of the intellect, which is significant and potentially correct, from the various transcendental systems of the universe, which are chimeras.

In both its parts, however, transcendentalism had much to recommend it to American philosophers, for the transcendental method appealed to the individualistic and revolutionary temper of their youth, while transcendental myths enabled them to find a new status for their inherited theology, and to give what parts of it they cared to preserve some semblance of philosophical backing. This last was the use to which the transcendental method was put by Kant himself, who first brought it into vogue, before the terrible weapon had got out of hand, and become the instrument of pure romanticism. Kant came, he himself said, to remove knowledge in order to make room for faith, which in his case meant faith in Calvinism. In other words, he applied the transcendental method to matters of fact, reducing them thereby to human ideas, in order to give to the Calvinistic postulates of conscience a metaphysical validity. For Kant had a genteel tradition of his own, which he wished to remove to a place of safety, feeling that the empirical world had become too hot for it; and this place of safety was the region of transcendental myth. I need hardly say how perfectly this expedient suited the needs of philosophers in America, and it is no accident if the influence of Kant soon became dominant here. To embrace this philosophy was regarded as a sign of profound metaphysical insight, although the most mediocre minds found no difficulty in embracing it. In truth it was a sign of having been brought up in the genteel tradition, of feeling it weak, and of wishing to save it.

But the transcendental method, in its way, was also sympathetic to the American mind. It embodied, in a radical form, the spirit of Protestantism as distinguished from its inherited doctrines; it was autonomous, undismayed, calmly revolutionary; it felt that Will was deeper than Intellect; it focussed everything here and now, and asked all things to show their credentials at the bar of the young self, and to prove their value for this latest born moment. These things are truly American; they would be characteristic of any young society with a keen and discursive intelligence, and they are strikingly exemplified in the thought and in the person of Emerson. They constitute what he called self-trust. Self-trust, like other transcendental attitudes, may be expressed in metaphysical fables. The romantic spirit may imagine itself to be an absolute force, evoking and moulding the plastic world to express its varying moods. But for a pioneer who is actually a world-builder this metaphysical illusion has a partial warrant in historical fact; far more warrant than it could boast of in the fixed and articulated society of Europe, among the moonstruck rebels and sulking poets of the romantic era. Emerson was a shrewd Yankee, by instinct on the winning side; he was a cheery, child-like soul, impervious to the evidence of evil, as of everything that it did not suit his transcendental individuality to appreciate or to notice. More, perhaps, than anybody that has ever lived, he practised the transcendental method in all its purity. He had no system. He opened his eyes on the world every morning with a fresh sincerity, marking how things seemed to him then, or what they suggested to his spontaneous fancy. This fancy, for being spontaneous, was not always novel; it was guided by the habits and training of his mind, which were those of a preacher. Yet he never insisted on his notions so as to turn them into settled dogmas; he felt in his bones that they were myths. Sometimes, indeed, the bad example of other transcendentalists, less true than he to their method, or the pressing questions of unintelligent people, or the instinct we all have to think our ideas final, led him to the very verge of system-making; but he stopped short. Had he made a system out of his notion of compensation, or the over-soul, or spiritual laws, the result would have been as thin and forced as it is in other transcendental systems. But he coveted truth; and he returned to experience, to history, to poetry, to the natural science of his day, for new starting-points and hints toward fresh transcendental musings.

To covet truth is a very distinguished passion. Every philosopher says he is pursuing the truth, but this is seldom the case. As Mr. Bertrand Russell has observed, one reason why philosophers often fail to reach the truth is that often they do not desire to reach it. Those who are genuinely concerned in discovering what happens to be true are rather the men of science, the naturalists, the historians; and ordinarily they discover it, according to their lights. The truths they find are never complete, and are not always important; but they are integral parts of the truth, facts and circumstances that help to fill in the picture, and that no later interpretation can invalidate or afford to contradict. But professional philosophers are usually only apologists: that is, they are absorbed in defending some vested illusion or some eloquent idea. Like lawyers or detectives, they study the case for which they are retained, to see how much evidence or semblance of evidence they can gather for the defence, and how much prejudice they can raise against the witnesses for the prosecution; for they know they are defending prisoners suspected by the world, and perhaps by their own good sense, of falsification. They do not covet truth, but victory and the dispelling of their own doubts. What they defend is some system, that is, some view about the totality of things, of which men are actually ignorant. No system would have ever been framed if people had been simply interested in knowing what is true, whatever it may be. What produces systems is the interest in maintaining against all comers that some favourite or inherited idea of ours is sufficient and right. A system may contain an account of many things which, in detail, are true enough; but as a system, covering infinite possibilities that neither our experience nor our logic can prejudge, it must be a work of imagination and a piece of human soliloquy. It may be expressive of human experience, it may be poetical; but how should any one who really coveted truth suppose that it was true?

Emerson had no system; and his coveting truth had another exceptional consequence: he was detached, unworldly, contemplative. When he came out of the conventicle or the reform meeting, or out of the rapturous close atmosphere of the lecture-room, he heard Nature whispering to him: "Why so hot, little sir?" No doubt the spirit or energy of the world is what is acting in us, as the sea is what rises in every little wave; but it passes through us, and cry out as we may, it will move on. Our privilege is to have perceived it as it moves. Our dignity is not in what we do, but in what we understand. The whole world is doing things. We are turning in that vortex; yet within us is silent observation, the speculative eye before which all passes, which bridges the distances and compares the combatants. On this side of his genius Emerson broke away from all conditions of age or country and represented nothing except intelligence itself.

There was another element in Emerson, curiously combined with transcendentalism, namely, his love and respect for Nature. Nature, for the transcendentalist, is precious because it is his own work, a mirror in which he looks at himself and says (like a poet relishing his own verses), "What a genius I am! Who would have thought there was such stuff in me?" And the philosophical egotist finds in his doctrine a ready explanation of whatever beauty and commodity nature actually has. No wonder, he says to himself, that nature is sympathetic, since I made it. And such a view, one-sided and even fatuous as it may be, undoubtedly sharpens the vision of a poet and a moralist to all that is inspiriting and symbolic in the natural world. Emerson was particularly ingenious and clear-sighted in feeling the spiritual uses of fellowship with the elements. This is something in which all Teutonic poetry is rich and which forms, I think, the most genuine and spontaneous part of modern taste, and especially of American taste. Just as some people are naturally enthralled and refreshed by music, so others are by landscape. Music and landscape make up the spiritual resources of those who cannot or dare not express their unfulfilled ideals in words. Serious poetry, profound religion (Calvinism, for instance), are the joys of an unhappiness that confesses itself; but when a genteel tradition forbids people to confess that they are unhappy, serious poetry and profound religion are closed to them by that; and since human life, in its depths, cannot then express itself openly, imagination is driven for comfort into abstract arts, where human circumstances are lost sight of, and human problems dissolve in a purer medium. The pressure of care is thus relieved, without its quietus being found in intelligence. To understand oneself is the classic form of consolation; to elude oneself is the romantic. In the presence of music or landscape human experience eludes itself; and thus roman-

ticism is the bond between transcendental and naturalistic sentiment. The winds and clouds come to minister to the solitary ego.

Have there been, we may ask, any successful efforts to escape
from the genteel tradition, and to express something worth expressing behind its back? This might well not have occurred as yet;
but America is so precocious, it has been trained by the genteel
tradition to be so wise for its years, that some indications of a truly
native philosophy and poetry are already to be found. I might mention the humorists, of whom you here in California have had your
share. The humorists, however, only half escape the genteel tradition; their humour would lose its savour if they had wholly escaped
it. They point to what contradicts it in the facts; but not in order
to abandon the genteel tradition, for they have nothing solid to put
in its place. When they point out how ill many facts fit into it, they
do not clearly conceive that this militates against the standard, but
think it a funny perversity in the facts. Of course, did they ear-
nestly respect the genteel tradition, such an incongruity would seem
to them sad, rather than ludicrous. Perhaps the prevalence of humour in America, in and out of season, may be taken as one more
evidence that the genteel tradition is present pervasively, but everywhere weak. Similarly in Italy, during the Renaissance, the Catholic
tradition could not be banished from the intellect, since there was
nothing articulate to take its place; yet its hold on the heart was
singularly relaxed. The consequence was that humorists could re-
gale themselves with the foibles of monks and of cardinals, with
the credulity of fools, and the bogus miracles of the saints; not
intending to deny the theory of the church, but caring for it so
little at heart that they could find it infinitely amusing that it should
be contradicted in men's lives and that no harm should come of it.
So when Mark Twain says, "I was born of poor but dishonest par-
ents," the humour depends on the parody of the genteel Anglo-
Saxon convention that it is disreputable to be poor; but to hint at
the hollowness of it would not be amusing if it did not remain at
bottom one's habitual conviction.

The one American writer who has left the genteel tradition entirely behind is perhaps Walt Whitman. For this reason educated
Americans find him rather an unpalatable person, who they sincerely protest ought not to be taken for a representative of their

culture; and he certainly should not, because their culture is so genteel and traditional. But the foreigner may sometimes think otherwise, since he is looking for what may have arisen in America to express, not the polite and conventional American mind, but the spirit and the inarticulate principles that animate the community, on which its own genteel mentality seems to sit rather lightly. When the foreigner opens the pages of Walt Whitman, he thinks that he has come at last upon something representative and original. In Walt Whitman democracy is carried into psychology and morals. The various sights, moods, and emotions are given each one vote; they are declared to be all free and equal, and the innumerable commonplace moments of life are suffered to speak like the others. Those moments formerly reputed great are not excluded, but they are made to march in the ranks with their companions—plain foot-soldiers and servants of the hour. Nor does the refusal to discriminate stop there; we must carry our principle further down, to the animals, to inanimate nature, to the cosmos as a whole. Whitman became a pantheist; but his pantheism, unlike that of the Stoics and of Spinoza, was unintellectual, lazy, and self-indulgent; for he simply felt jovially that everything real was good enough, and that he was good enough himself. In him Bohemia rebelled against the genteel tradition; but the reconstruction that alone can justify revolution did not ensue. His attitude, in principle, was utterly disintegrating; his poetic genius fell back to the lowest level, perhaps, to which it is possible for poetic genius to fall. He reduced his imagination to a passive sensorium for the registering of impressions. No element of construction remained in it, and therefore no element of penetration. But his scope was wide; and his lazy, desultory apprehension was poetical. His work, for the very reason that it is so rudimentary, contains a beginning, or rather many beginnings, that might possibly grow into a noble moral imagination, a worthy filling for the human mind. An American in the nineteenth century who completely disregarded the genteel tradition could hardly have done more.

But there is another distinguished man, lately lost to this country, who has given some rude shocks to this tradition and who, as much as Whitman, may be regarded as representing the genuine, the long silent American mind—I mean William James. He and his brother Henry were as tightly swaddled in the genteel tradition as any infant geniuses could be, for they were born before 1850, and in a Swedenborgian household. Yet they burst those bands almost entirely. The ways in which the two brothers freed themselves, however, are interestingly different. Mr. Henry James has done it by adopting the point of view of the outer world, and by turning the genteel American tradition, as he turns everything else, into a subject-matter for analysis. For him it is a curious habit of mind, intimately comprehended, to be compared with other habits of mind, also well known to him. Thus he has overcome the genteel tradition in the classic way, by understanding it. With William James too this infusion of worldly insight and European sympathies was a potent influence, especially in his earlier days; but the chief source of his liberty was another. It was his personal spontaneity, similar to that of Emerson, and his personal vitality, similar to that of nobody else. Convictions and ideas came to him, so to speak, from the subsoil. He had a prophetic sympathy with the dawning sentiments of the age, with the moods of the dumb majority. His scattered words caught fire in many parts of the world. His way of thinking and feeling represented the true America, and represented in a measure the whole ultra-modern, radical world. Thus he eluded the genteel tradition in the romantic way, by continuing it into its opposite. The romantic mind, glorified in Hegel's dialectic (which is not dialectic at all, but a sort of tragi-comic history of experience), is always rendering its thoughts unrecognisable through the infusion of new insights, and through the insensible transformation of the moral feeling that accompanies them, till at last it has completely reversed its old judgments under cover of expanding them. Thus the genteel tradition was led a merry dance when it fell again into the hands of a genuine and vigorous romanticist like William James. He restored their revolutionary force to its neutralised elements, by picking them out afresh, and emphasising them separately, according to his personal predilections.

For one thing, William James kept his mind and heart wide open to all that might seem, to polite minds, odd, personal, or visionary in religion and philosophy. He gave a sincerely respectful hearing to sentimentalists, mystics, spiritualists, wizards, cranks, quacks, and impostors—for it is hard to draw the line, and James was not willing to draw it prematurely. He thought, with his usual modesty, that any of these might have something to teach him. The lame, the halt, the blind, and those speaking with tongues could come to him with the certainty of finding sympathy; and if they were not healed, at least they were comforted, that a famous professor should take them so seriously; and they began to feel that after all to have only one leg, or one hand, or one eye, or to have three, might be in itself no less beauteous than to have just two, like the stolid majority. Thus William James became the friend and helper of those groping, nervous, half-educated, spiritually disinherited, passionately hungry individuals of which America is full. He became, at the same time, their spokesman and representative before the learned world; and he made it a chief part of his vocation to recast what the learned world has to offer, so that as far as possible it might serve the needs and interests of these people.

Yet the normal practical masculine American, too, had a friend in William James. There is a feeling abroad now, to which biology and Darwinism lend some colour, that theory is simply an instrument for practice, and intelligence merely a help toward material survival. Bears, it is said, have fur and claws, but poor naked man is condemned to be intelligent, or he will perish. This feeling William James embodied in that theory of thought and of truth which he called pragmatism. Intelligence, he thought, is no miraculous, idle faculty, by which we mirror passively any or everything that happens to be true, reduplicating the real world to no purpose. Intelligence has its roots and its issue in the context of events; it is one kind of practical adjustment, an experimental act, a form of vital tension. It does not essentially serve to picture other parts of reality, but to connect them. This view was not worked out by William James in its psychological and historical details; unfortunately he developed it chiefly in controversy against its opposite, which he called intellectualism, and which he hated with all the hatred of which his kind heart was capable. Intellectualism, as he conceived it, was pure pedantry; it impoverished and verbalised everything, and tied up nature in red tape. Ideas and rules that may have been occasionally useful it put in the place of the full-blooded irrational movement of life which had called them into being; and these abstractions, so soon obsolete, it strove to fix and to worship for ever. Thus all creeds and theories and all formal precepts sink in the estimation of the pragmatist to a local and temporary grammar of action; a grammar that must be changed slowly by time, and may be changed quickly by genius. To know things as a whole, or as they are eternally, if there is anything eternal in them, is not only beyond our powers, but would prove worthless, and perhaps even fatal to our lives. Ideas are not mirrors, they are weapons; their function is to prepare us to meet events, as future experience may unroll them. Those ideas that disappoint us are false ideas; those to which events are true are true themselves.

This may seem a very utilitarian view of the mind; and I confess I think it a partial one, since the logical force of beliefs and ideas, their truth or falsehood as assertions, has been overlooked altogether, or confused with the vital force of the material processes which these ideas express. It is an external view only, which marks the place and conditions of the mind in nature, but neglects its specific essence; as if a jewel were defined as a round hole in a ring. Nevertheless, the more materialistic the pragmatist's theory of the mind is, the more vitalistic his theory of nature will have to become. If the intellect is a device produced in organic bodies to expedite their processes, these organic bodies must have interests and a chosen direction in their life; otherwise their life could not be expedited, nor could anything be useful to it. In other words— and this is a third point at which the philosophy of William James has played havoc with the genteel tradition, while ostensibly defending it—nature must be conceived anthropomorphically and in psychological terms. Its purposes are not to be static harmonies, self-unfolding destinies, the logic of spirit, the spirit of logic, or any other formal method and abstract law; its purposes are to be concrete endeavours, finite efforts of souls living in an environment which they transform and by which they, too, are affected. A spirit, the divine spirit as much as the human, as this new animism conceives it, is a romantic adventurer. Its future is undetermined. Its scope, its duration, and the quality of its life are all contingent. This spirit grows; it buds and sends forth feelers, sounding the depths around for such other centres of force or life as may exist there. It has a vital momentum, but no predetermined goal. It uses its past as a stepping-stone, or rather as a divingboard, but has an absolutely fresh will at each moment to plunge this way or that into the unknown. The universe is an experiment; it is unfinished.

It has no ultimate or total nature, because it has no end. It embodies no formula or statable law; any formula is at best a poor abstraction, describing what, in some region and for some time, may be the most striking characteristic of existence; the law is a description *a posteriori* of the habit things have chosen to acquire, and which they may possibly throw off altogether. What a day may bring forth is uncertain; uncertain even to God. Omniscience is impossible; time is real; what had been omniscience hitherto might discover something more to-day. "There shall be news," William James was fond of saying with rapture, quoting from the unpublished poem of an obscure friend, "there shall be news in heaven!" There is almost certainly, he thought, a God now; there may be several gods, who might exist together, or one after the other. We might, by our conspiring sympathies, help to make a new one. Much in us is doubtless immortal; we survive death for some time in a recognisable form; but what our career and transformations may be in the sequel we cannot tell, although we may help to determine them by our daily choices. Observation must be continual if our ideas are to remain true. Eternal vigilance is the price of knowledge; perpetual hazard, perpetual experiment keep quick the edge of life.

This is, so far as I know, a new philosophical vista; it is a conception never before presented, although implied, perhaps, in various quarters, as in Norse and even Greek mythology. It is a vision radically empirical and radically romantic; and as William James himself used to say, the visions and not the arguments of a philosopher are the interesting and influential things about him. William James, rather too generously, attributed this vision to M. Bergson, and regarded him in consequence as a philosopher of the first rank, whose thought was to be one of the turning-points in history. M. Bergson had killed intellectualism. It was his book on creative evolution, said James with humorous emphasis, that had come at last to *"écraser l'infâme."* We may suspect, notwithstanding, that intellectualism, infamous and crushed, will survive the blow; and if the author of the Book of Ecclesiastes were now alive, and heard that there shall be news in heaven, he would doubtless say that there may possibly be news there, but that under the sun there is nothing new—not even radical empiricism or radical romanticism, which from the beginning of the world has been the philosophy of those who as yet had had little experience; for to the blinking little child it is not merely something in the world that is new daily, but everything is new all day.

I am not concerned with the rights and wrongs of that controversy; my point is only that William James, in this genial evolutionary view of the world, has given a rude shock to the genteel tradition. What! The world a gradual improvisation? Creation unpremeditated? God a sort of young poet or struggling artist? William James is an advocate of theism; pragmatism adds one to the evidences of religion; that is excellent. But is not the cool abstract piety of the genteel getting more than it asks for? This empirical naturalistic God is too crude and positive a force; he will work miracles, he will answer prayers, he may inhabit distinct places, and have distinct conditions under which alone he can operate; he is a neighbouring being, whom we can act upon, and rely upon for specific aids, as upon a personal friend, or a physician, or an insurance company. How disconcerting! Is not this new theology a little like superstition? And yet how interesting, how exciting, if it should happen to be true! I am far from wishing to suggest that such a view seems to me more probable than conventional idealism or than Christian orthodoxy. All three are in the region of dramatic system-making and myth to which probabilities are irrelevant. If one man says the moon is sister to the sun, and another that she is his daughter, the question is not which notion is more probable, but whether either of them is at all expressive. The so-called evidences are devised afterwards, when faith and imagination have prejudged the issue. The force of William James's new theology, or romantic cosmology, lies only in this: that it has broken the spell of the genteel tradition, and enticed faith in a new direction, which on second thoughts may prove no less alluring than the old. The important fact is not that the new fancy might possibly be true —who shall know that?—but that it has entered the heart of a leading American to conceive and to cherish it. The genteel tradition cannot be dislodged by these insurrections; there are circles to which it is still congenial, and where it will be preserved. But it has been challenged and (what is perhaps more insidious) it has been discovered. No one need be browbeaten any longer into accepting it. No one need be afraid, for instance, that his fate is sealed because some young prig may call him a dualist; the pint would call the quart a dualist, if you tried to pour the quart into him. We need not be afraid of being less profound, for being direct and sincere. The intellectual world may be traversed in many directions; the whole has not been surveyed; there is a great career in it open to talent. That is a sort of knell, that tolls the passing of the genteel tradition. Something else is now in the field; something else can appeal to the imagination, and be a thousand times more idealistic than academic idealism, which is often simply a way of white-washing and adoring things as they are. The illegitimate monopoly which the genteel tradition had established over what ought to be assumed and what ought to be hoped for has been broken down by the first-born of the family, by the genius of the race. Henceforth there can hardly be the same peace and the same pleasure in hugging the old proprieties. Hegel will be to the next generation what Sir William Hamilton was to the last. Nothing will have been disproved, but everything will have been abandoned. An honest man has spoken, and the cant of the genteel tradition has become harder for young lips to repeat.

With this I have finished such a sketch as I am here able to offer you of the genteel tradition in American philosophy. The subject is complex, and calls for many an excursus and qualifying footnote; yet I think the main outlines are clear enough. The chief fountains of this tradition were Calvinism and transcendentalism. Both were living fountains; but to keep them alive they required, one an agonised conscience, and the other a radical subjective criticism of knowledge. When these rare metaphysical preoccupations disappeared—and the American atmosphere is not favourable to either of them—the two systems ceased to be inwardly understood; they subsisted as sacred mysteries only; and the combination of the two in some transcendental system of the universe (a contradiction in principle) was doubly artificial. Besides, it could hardly be held with a single mind. Natural science, history, the beliefs implied in labour and invention, could not be disregarded altogether; so that the transcendental philosopher was condemned to a double allegiance, and to not letting his left hand know the bluff that his right hand was making. Nevertheless, the difficulty in bringing practical inarticulate convictions to expression is very great, and the genteel tradition has subsisted in the academic mind for want of anything equally academic to take its place.

The academic mind, however, has had its flanks turned. On the one side came the revolt of the Bohemian temperament, with its poetry of crude naturalism; on the other side came an impassioned empiricism, welcoming popular religious witnesses to the unseen, reducing science to an instrument of success in action, and declaring the universe to be wild and young, and not to be harnessed by the logic of any school.

This revolution, I should think, might well find an echo among you, who live in a thriving society, and in the presence of a virgin and prodigious world. When you transform nature to your uses, when you experiment with her forces, and reduce them to industrial agents, you cannot feel that nature was made by you or for you, for then these adjustments would have been pre-established. Much less can you feel it when she destroys your labour of years in a momentary spasm. You must feel, rather, that you are an offshoot of her life; one brave little force among her immense forces. When you escape, as you love to do, to your forests and your sierras, I am sure again that you do not feel you made them, or that they were made for you. They have grown, as you have grown, only more massively and more slowly. In their non-human beauty and peace they stir the sub-human depths and the superhuman possibilities of your own spirit. It is no transcendental logic that they teach; and they give no sign of any deliberate morality seated in the world. It is rather the vanity and superficiality of all logic, the needlessness of argument, the relativity of morals, the strength of time, the fertility of matter, the variety, the unspeakable variety, of possible life. Everything is measurable and conditioned, indefinitely repeated, yet, in repetition, twisted somewhat from its old form. Everywhere is beauty and nowhere permanence, everywhere an incipient harmony, nowhere an intention, nor a responsibility, nor a plan. It is the irresistible suasion of this daily spectacle, it is the daily discipline of contact with things, so different from the verbal discipline of the schools, that will, I trust, inspire the philosophy of your children. A Californian whom I had recently the pleasure of meeting observed that, if the philosophers had lived among your mountains their systems would have been different from what they are. Certainly, I should say, very different from what those systems are which the European genteel tradition has handed down since Socrates; for these systems are egotistical; directly or indirectly they are anthropocentric, and inspired by the conceited notion that man, or human reason, or the human distinction between good and evil, is the centre and pivot of the universe. That is what the mountains and the woods should make you at last ashamed to assert. From what, indeed, does the society of nature liberate you, that you find it so sweet? It is hardly (is it?) that you wish to forget your past, or your friends, or that you have any secret contempt for your present ambitions. You respect these, you respect them perhaps too much; you are not suffered by the genteel tradition to criticise or to reform them at all radically. No; it is the yoke of this genteel tradition itself that these primeval solitudes lift from your shoulders. They suspend your forced sense of your own importance not merely as individuals, but even as men. They allow you, in one happy moment, at once to play and to worship, to take yourselves simply, humbly, for what you are, and to salute the wild, indifferent, noncensorious infinity of nature. You are admonished that what you can do avails little materially, and in the end nothing. At the same time, through wonder and pleasure, you are taught speculation. You learn what you are really fitted to do, and where lie your natural dignity and joy, namely, in representing many things, without being them, and in letting your imagination, through sympathy, celebrate and echo their life. Because the peculiarity of man is that his machinery for reaction on external things has involved an imaginative transcript of these things, which is preserved and suspended in his fancy; and the interest and beauty of this inward landscape, rather than any fortunes that may await his body in the outer world, constitute his proper happiness. By their mind, its scope, quality, and temper, we estimate men, for by the mind only do we exist as men, and are more than so many storage-batteries for material energy. Let us therefore be frankly human. Let us be content to live in the mind.

7 / THE REVOLT AGAINST FORMALISM IN CRITICISM

Joel E. Spingarn was born in 1875 and attended Columbia University, where he took his bachelor's degree in 1895 and Ph.D. in 1899. He served in the English Department at Columbia University from 1899 to 1911, when he resigned in protest over an issue of academic freedom. Spingarn was active in politics, progressive in sentiment, an unsuccessful candidate for Congress in 1908, and a delegate to the Progressive national conventions in 1912 and 1916. He served as chairman of the NAACP from 1913 to 1919 and was its president from 1931 to 1939. He was also one of the founders of and a literary adviser to the publishing house of Harcourt, Brace and Company. ¶The following selection, "The New Criticism," was a lecture delivered at Columbia on March 9, 1910. Spingarn was the first to use the phrase "New Criticism" to describe a school of critics. Although his ideas were not the same as those of the "New Critics" of the 1930's, his was a pioneer effort to give new freedom for literary experimentation and a new dignity to criticism. This essay is not only a statement of the general principles of creative criticism, but also a ferocious attack on most of the time-honored methods of critical procedure.

II

The theory of expression, the concept of literature as an art of expression, is the common ground on which critics have met for

SOURCE: Joel Elias Spingarn, "The New Criticism," Chapter I in *Creative Criticism: Essays on the Unity of Genius and Taste* (New York: Henry Holt and Co., 1917), pp. 3-44.

a century or more. Yet how many absurdities, how many complicated systems, how many confusions have been superimposed on this fundamental idea; and how slowly has its full significance become the possession of critics! To accept the naked principle is to play havoc with these confusions and complications; and no one has seen this more clearly, or driven home its inevitable consequences with more intelligence and vigor, than an Italian thinker and critic of our own day, Benedetto Croce, who has been gaining ground in the English-speaking world from the day when Mr. Balfour several years ago gave him a kind of official introduction in his Romanes Lecture. But I for one needed no introduction to his work; under his banner I enrolled myself long ago, and here re-enroll myself in what I now say. He has led esthetic thought inevitably from the concept that art is expression to the conclusion that all expression is art. Time does not permit, nor reason ask, that we should follow this argument through all its *pros* and *cons*. If this theory of expression be once and for all accepted, as indeed it has been partly though confusedly, accepted by all modern critics, the ground of Criticism is cleared of its dead lumber and its weeds. I propose now merely to point out this dead lumber and these weeds. In other words, we shall see to what conclusions the critical thought and practice of a century have been inevitably converging, and what elements of the old Criticism and the old literary history are disappearing from the new.

In the first place, we have done with all the old Rules. The very conception of "rules" harks back to an age of magic, and reminds the modern of those mysterious words which the heroes of the fairy-tales are without reason forbidden to utter; the rules are a survival of the savage *taboo*. We find few arbitrary rules in Aristotle, who limited himself to empirical inductions from the experience of literature; but they appear in the later Greek rhetoricians; and in the Romans, empirical induction has been hardened into dogma. Horace lays down the law to the prospective playwright in this manner: "You must never have more than three actors on the stage at any one time; you must never let your drama have more or less than five acts." It is unnecessary to trace the history of these rules, or to indicate how they increased in number, how they were arranged into a system by the classicists of the sixteenth and seventeenth centuries, and how they burdened the creative art of that period. They were never without their enemies. We have seen how Aretino was pitted against Scaliger, Saint-Evremond against Boileau; and in every age the poets have astounded the critics by transgressing rules without the sacrifice of beauty; but it was not until the end of the eighteenth century that the Romanticists banished them from the province of Criticism. The pedantry of our own day has borrowed "conventions" from history and "technique" from science as substitutes for the outworn formulæ of the past; but these are merely new names for the old mechanical rules; and they too will go, when Criticism clearly recognizes in every work of art a spiritual creation governed by its own law.

We have done with the *genres,* or literary kinds. Their history is inseparably bound up with that of the classical rules. Certain works of literature have a general resemblance and are loosely classed together (for the sake of convenience) as lyric, comedy, tragedy, epic, pastoral, and the like; the classicists made of each of these divisions a fixed norm governed by inviolable laws. The separation of the *genres* was a consequence of this law of classicism: comedy should not be mingled with tragedy, nor epic with lyric. But no sooner was the law enunciated than it was broken by an artist impatient or ignorant of its restraints, and the critics have been obliged to explain away these violations of their laws, or gradually to change the laws themselves. But if art is organic expression, and every work of art is to be interrogated with the question, "What has it expressed, and how completely?" there is no place for the question whether it has conformed to some convenient classification of critics or to some law derived from this classification. The lyric, the pastoral, the epic, are abstractions without concrete reality in the world of art. Poets do not really write epics, pastorals, lyrics, however much they may be deceived by these false abstractions; they express themselves, and this expression is their only form. There are not, therefore, only three, or ten, or a hundred literary kinds; there are as many kinds as there are individual poets. But it is in the field of literary history that this error is most obvious. Shakespeare wrote *King Lear, Venus and Adonis,* and a sequence of sonnets. What becomes of Shakespeare, the creative artist, when these three works are separated from one another by the historian of poetry; when they lose their connection with his single creative soul, and are classified with other works with which they have only a loose and vague relation? To slice up the history of English literature into compartments marked comedy, tragedy, lyric, and the like, is to be guilty of a complete misunderstanding of the meaning of Criticism; and literary history becomes a logical absurdity when its data are not organically related but cut up into sections, and placed in such compartments as these. Only in one sense has any of these terms any profound significance, and that is the use of the word "lyric" to represent the free expressiveness of art. All art is lyrical,—the *Divine Comedy, King Lear,* Rodin's "Thinker," the Parthenon, a Corot landscape, a Bach fugue, or Isadora Duncan's dancing, as much as the songs of Heine or Shelley.

We have done with the comic, the tragic, the sublime, and an army of vague abstractions of their kind. These have grown out of the generalizations of the Alexandrian critics, acquiring a new lease of life in the eighteenth century. Gray and his friend West corresponded with each other on the subject of the sublime; later, Schiller distinguished between the naïve and the sentimental; Jean Paul defined humor, and Hegel defined the tragic. If these terms represent the content of art, they may be relegated to the same category as joy, hate, sorrow, enthusiasm; and we should speak of the comic in the same general way in which we might speak of the expression of joy in a poem. If, on the other hand, these terms represent abstract classifications of poetry, their use in criticism sins against the very nature of art. Every poet re-expresses the universe in his own way, and every poem is a new and independent expression. The tragic does not exist for Criticism, but only Æschylus and Calderón, Shakespeare and Racine. There is no objection to the use of the word tragic as a convenient label for somewhat similar poems, but to find laws for the tragic and to test creative artists by such laws as these is simply to give a more abstract form to the outworn classical conception of dramatic rules.

We have done with the theory of style, with metaphor, simile, and all the paraphernalia of Græco-Roman rhetoric. These owe their existence to the assumption that style is separate from expression, that it is something which may be added or subtracted at will from the work of art, a flourish of the pen, an external embellishment, instead of the poet's individual vision of reality, the music of his whole manner of being. But we know that art *is* expression, that it is complete in itself, that to alter it is to create another expression and therefore to create another work of art. If the poet, for example, says of springtime that " 'Tis now the blood runs gold," he has not employed a substitute for something else, such as "the blood tingles in our veins"; he has expressed his thought in its completeness, and there is no equivalent for his expression except itself.

> Each perfect in its place; and each content
> With that perfection which its being meant.

Such expressions are still called metaphors in the text-books; but metaphor, simile, and all the old terms of classical rhetoric are signs of the zodiac, magical incantations, astrological formulæ, interesting only to antiquarian curiosity. To Montaigne they suggested "the prattle of chambermaids"; to me they suggest rather the drone and singsong of many schoolmistresses. We still hear talk of the "grand style," and essays on style continue to be written, like the old "arts of poetry" of two centuries ago. But the theory of styles has no longer a real place in modern thought; we have learned that it is no less impossible to study style as separate from the work of art than to study the comic as separate from the work of the comic artist.

We have done with all moral judgment of art as art. Horace said that pleasure and profit are the function or end of poetry, and for many centuries the critics quarreled over the terms "pleasure" and "profit." Some said that poetry was meant to instruct; some, merely to please; some, to do both. Romantic criticism first enunciated the principle that art has no aim except expression; that its aim is complete when expression is complete; that "beauty is its own excuse for being." It is not the inherent function of poetry to further any moral or social cause, any more than it is the function of bridge-building to further the cause of Esperanto. The historian, the philosopher, the legislator, may consider a work of art, not as a work of art, but as a social document, just as the quarryman may consider a statue merely as so many pounds of marble, but in so doing they ignore its essential purpose and the fundamental source of its power. For if the achievement of the poet be to express any material he may select, and to express it with a completeness that we recognize as perfection, obviously morals can play no part in the judgment which Criticism may form of this artistic achievement. To say that poetry, as poetry, is moral or immoral is as meaningless as to say that an equilateral triangle is moral and an isosceles triangle immoral, or to speak of the immorality of a musical chord or a Gothic arch. It is only conceivable in a world in which dinner-table conversation runs after this fashion: "This cauliflower would be good if it had only been prepared in accordance with international law." "Do you know why my cook's pastry is so good? Because he has never told a lie or seduced a woman." We do not concern ourselves with morals when we test the engineer's bridge or the scientist's researches; indeed we go farther, and say that it is the moral duty of the scientist to disregard any theory of morals in his search for truth. Beauty's world is remote from both these standards; she aims neither at morals nor at truth. Her imaginary creations, by definition, make no pretense to reality, and cannot be judged by reality's tests. The poet's only moral duty, as a poet, is to be true to his art, and to express his vision of reality as well as he can. If the ideals enunciated by poets are not those which we admire most, we must blame not the poets but ourselves: in the world where morals count we have failed to give them the proper material out of which to rear a nobler edifice. In so far as this is inherent in the nature of our humanity, it is not affected by the special conditions of any single society in space and time: though art is a symbol of the eternal conflict between aspiration and reality, it must at the same time remain forever a symbol of mortal imperfection. Critics everywhere except in America have ceased to test literature by the standards of ethics, and recognize in art an inevitable expression of a side of man's nature that can find no other realization except in it.

We have done with the confusion between the drama and the theater which has permeated dramatic criticism for over half a century. The theory that the drama is not a creative art, but a mere product of the physical exigencies of the theater, is as old as the sixteenth century. An Italian scholar of that age was the first to maintain that plays are intended to be acted on a stage, under certain restricted physical conditions, and before a large and hetero-geneous crowd; dramatic performance has developed out of these conditions, and the test of its excellence is therefore the pleasure it gives to the mixed audience that supports it. This idea was taken hold of by some of the German romanticists, for the purpose of justifying the Shakespearean drama in its apparent divergence from the classical "rules." Shakespeare cannot be judged by the rules of the Greek theater (so ran their argument), for the drama is an inevitable product of theatrical conditions; these conditions in Elizabethan England were not the same as those of Periclean Athens; and it is therefore absurd to judge Shakespeare's practice by that of Sophocles. Here at least the idea helped to bring Shakespeare home to many new hearts by ridding the age of mistaken prejudices, and served a useful purpose, as a specious argument may persuade men to contribute to a noble work, or a mad fanatic may rid the world of a tyrant. But with this achievement its usefulness but not its life was ended. It has been developed into a system, and become a dogma of dramatic critics; it is our contemporary equivalent for the "rules" of seventeenth-century pedantry. As a matter of fact, the dramatic artist is to be judged by no other standard than that applied to any other creative artist: what has he tried to express, and how has he expressed it? It is true that the theater is not only an art but a business, and the so-called "success" of a play is of vital interest to the theater in so far as it is a commercial undertaking. "The success may justify the playwright," said an old French critic, "but it may not be so easy to justify the success." The test of "success" is an economic test, and concerns not art or the criticism of art, but political economy. Valuable contributions to economic and social history have been made by students who have investigated the changing conditions of the theater and the vicissitudes of taste on the part of theatrical audiences; but these have the same relation to Criticism, and to the drama as an art, that a history of the publisher's trade and its influence on the personal fortunes of poets would bear to the history of poetry.

We have done with technique as separate from art. It has been pointed out that style cannot be disassociated from art; and the false air of science which the term "technique" seems to possess should not blind us to the fact that it too involves the same error. "Technique is really personality; that is the reason why the artist cannot teach it, why the pupil cannot learn it, and why the esthetic critic can understand it," says Oscar Wilde, in a dialogue on "The

Critic as Artist," which, amid much perversity and paradox, is illumined by many flashes of strange insight. The technique of poetry cannot be separated from its inner nature. Versification cannot be studied by itself, except loosely and for convenience; it remains always an inherent quality of the single poem. No two poets ever write in the same metre. Milton's line:

> These my sky-robes spun out of Iris' woof

is called an iambic pentameter; but it is not true that artistically it has something in common with every other line possessing the same succession of syllables and accents; in this sense it is not an iambic pentameter; it is only one thing; it is the line:

> These my sky-robes spun out of Iris' woof.

We have done with the history and criticism of poetic themes. It is possible to speak loosely of the handling of such a theme as Prometheus by Æschylus and by Shelley, of the story of Francesca da Rimini by Dante, Stephen Phillips, and D'Annunzio, or the story of King Arthur by Malory and Tennyson; but strictly speaking, they are not employing the same theme at all. Each artist is expressing a certain material and labeling it with an historic name. For Shelley Prometheus is only a label; he is expressing his artistic conception of life, not the history of a Greek Titan. It is the vital flame he has breathed into his work that makes it what it is, and with this vital flame (and not with labels) the critic should concern himself in the works of poets. The same answer must be given to those critics who insist on the use of contemporary material in poetry, and praise the poets whose subjects are drawn from the life of our own time. But even if it were possible for critics to determine in advance the subject-matter of poetry or to impose subjects on poets, how can a poet deal with anything but contemporary material? How can a twentieth-century poet, even when he imagines that he is concerned with Greek or Egyptian life, deal with any subject but the life of his own time, except in the most external and superficial detail? Cynics have said since the first outpourings of men's hearts, "There is nothing new in art; there are no new subjects." But the very reverse is true. There are no old subjects; every subject is new as soon as it has been transformed by the imagination of the poet.

We have done with the race, the time, the environment of a poet's work as an element in Criticism. To study these phases of a work of art is to treat it as an historic or social document, and the result is a contribution to the history of culture or civilization, with only a subsidiary interest for the history of art. We are not here concerned with the value of such studies as empirical preparations or concomitants, but only in their relation to the essential and inherent nature of the critical act. "Granted the times, the environment, the race, the passions of the poet, what has he done with his materials, how has he converted poetry out of reality?" To answer this question of the Italian De Sanctis as it refers to each single work of art is to perform what is truly the critic's vital function; this is to interpret "expression" in its rightful sense, and to liberate esthetic Criticism from the vassalage to *Kulturgeschichte* imposed on it by the school of Taine.

We have done with the "evolution" of literature. The concept of progress was first applied to literature in the seventeenth century, but at the very outset Pascal pointed out that a distinction must here be made between science and art; that science advances by accumulation of knowledge, while the changes of art cannot be reduced to any theory of progress. As a matter of fact, the theory involves the ranking of poets according to some arbitrary conception of their value; and the ranking of writers in order of merit has become obsolete, except in the "hundred best books" of the last decade and the "five-foot shelves" of yesterday. The later nineteenth century gave a new air of verisimilitude to this old theory by borrowing the term "evolution" from science; but this too involves a fundamental misconception of the free and original movement of art. A similar misconception is involved in the study of the "origins" of art; for art has no origin separate from man's life.

> In climes beyond the solar road,
> Where shaggy forms o'er ice-built mountains roam,
> The Muse has broke the twilight-gloom;

but though she wore savage raiment, she was no less the Muse. Art is simple at times, complex at others, but it is always art. The simple art of early times may be studied with profit; but the researches of anthropology have no vital significance for Criticism, unless the anthropologist studies the simplest forms of art in the same spirit as its highest; that is, unless the anthropologist is an esthetic critic.

Finally, we have done with the old rupture between genius and taste. When Criticism first propounded as its real concern the oft-repeated question: "What has the poet tried to express and how has he expressed it?" Criticism prescribed for itself the only possible method. How can the critic answer this question without becoming (if only for a moment of supreme power) at one with the creator? That is to say, taste must reproduce the work of art within itself in order to understand and judge it; and at that moment esthetic judgment becomes nothing more nor less than creative art itself. The identity of genius and taste is the final achievement of modern thought on the subject of art, and it means that fundamentally, in their most significant moments, the creative and the critical instincts are one and the same. From Goethe to Carlyle, from Carlyle to Arnold, from Arnold to Symons, there has been much talk of the "creative function" of Criticism. For each of these men the phrase held a different content; for Arnold it meant merely that Criticism creates the intellectual atmosphere of the age,—a social function of high importance, perhaps, yet wholly independent of esthetic significance. But the ultimate truth toward which these men were tending was more radical than that, and plays havoc with all the old platitudes about the sterility of taste. Criticism at last can free itself of its age-long self-contempt, now that it may realize that esthetic judgment and artistic creation are instinct with the same vital life. This identity does not sum up the whole life of the complex and difficult art of Criticism; but it is this identity which has been lost sight of and needs most emphasis now, for without it Criticism would really be impossible. "Genius is to esthetics what the ego is to philosophy, the only supreme and absolute reality," said Schelling; and without subduing the mind to this transcendental system, it remains true that what must always be inexplicable to mere reflection is just what gives power to poetry; that intellectual curiosity may amuse itself by asking its little questions of the silent sons of light, but they vouchsafe no answer to art's pale shadow, thought; the gods are kind if they give up their secret in another work of art, the art of Criticism, that serves as some sort of mirror to the art of literature, only because in their flashes of insight taste and genius are one.

8 / THE FAILURE OF PRAGMATISM

Although Randolph Bourne died at the age of thirty-two, he had a remarkable impact on American letters. Born in 1886, he took a master's degree from Columbia in 1913 and studied in London and Paris during 1913 and 1914. His literary career began in 1911 when he wrote for the Atlantic Monthly *and became contributing editor for the* Seven Arts *and* The Dial. *Also, he served on the staff of the* New Republic *from its beginning. Inspired by William James, John Dewey, and the social reformers of the day, he dreamt of a fellowship of the youth of America who shared the new enlightened ideas, who would bring about the great revolutionary departure in our life, a league of youth whose purpose was to create out of the chaos of American society a fine, free cultural order. The failure of liberal pragmatism to meet the issues raised by the First World War led him to write "The Twilight of Idols," which is not merely an attack on particular pragmatists and social reformers, but a critique of the limits of pragmatism as a basis for the new cultural freedom.*

III

It may seem unfair to group Professor Dewey with Mr. Spargo and Mr. Gompers, Mr. A. M. Simons,[1] and the Vigilantes. I do so only

[1] John Spargo, author of *The Bitter Cry of Children* (1905) and *Applied Socialism* (1912), who in 1917 resigned from the Socialist Party because of its criticism of Wilson's war policy; Samuel Gompers, since 1886 president of the American Federation of Labor; Algie M. Simons, socialist historian, author of *Social Forces in American History* (1911).

SOURCE: Randolph S. Bourne, "Twilight of Idols," Chapter 6, in Carl Resek, ed., *War and the Intellectual: Essays by Randolph S. Bourne 1915-1919* (New York: Harper & Row, Inc., 1964), pp. 53-64.

because in their acceptance of the war, they are all living out that popular American "instrumental" philosophy which Professor Dewey has formulated in such convincing and fascinating terms. On an infinitely more intelligent plane, he is yet one with them in his confidence that the war is motivated by democratic ends and is being made to serve them. A high mood of confidence and self-righteousness moves them all, a keen sense of control over events that makes them eligible to discipleship under Professor Dewey's philosophy. They are all hostile to impossibilism, to apathy, to any attitude that is not a cheerful and brisk setting to work to use the emergency to consolidate the gains of democracy. Not, Is it being used? but, Let us make a flutter about using it! This unanimity of mood puts the resenter of war out of the arena. But he can still seek to explain why this philosophy which has no place for the inexorable should have adjusted itself so easily to the inexorable of war, and why, although a philosophy of the creative intelligence in using means toward ends, it should show itself so singularly impoverished in its present supply of democratic values.

What is the matter with the philosophy? One has a sense of having come to a sudden, short stop at the end of an intellectual era. In the crisis, this philosophy of intelligent control just does not measure up to our needs. What is the root of this inadequacy that is felt so keenly by our restless minds? Van Wyck Brooks has pointed out searchingly the lack of poetic vision in our pragmatist "awakeners." Is there something in these realistic attitudes that works actually against poetic vision, against concern for the quality of life as above machinery of life? Apparently there is. The war has revealed a younger intelligentsia, trained up in the pragmatic dispensation, immensely ready for the executive ordering of events, pitifully unprepared for the intellectual interpretation or the idealistic focussing of ends. The young men in Belgium, the officers' training corps, the young men being sucked into the councils at Washington and into war-organization everywhere, have among them a definite element, upon whom Dewey, as veteran philosopher, might well bestow a papal blessing. They have absorbed the secret of scientific method as applied to political administration. They are liberal, enlightened, aware. They are touched with creative intelligence toward the solution of political and industrial problems. They are a wholly new force in American life, the product of the swing in the colleges from a training that emphasized classical studies to one that emphasized political and economic values. Practically all this element, one would say, is lined up in service of the war-technique. There seems to have been a peculiar congeniality between the war and these men. It is as if the war and they had been waiting for each other. One wonders what scope they would have had for their intelligence without it. Probably most of them would have gone into industry and devoted themselves to sane reorganization schemes. What is significant is that it is the technical side of the war that appeals to them, not the interpretative or political side. The formulation of values and ideals, the production of articulate and suggestive thinking, had not, in their education, kept pace, to any extent whatever, with their technical aptitude. The result is that the field of intellectual formulation is very poorly manned by this younger intelligentsia. While they organize the war, formulation of opinion is left largely in the hands of professional patriots, sensational editors, archaic radicals. The intellectual work of this younger intelligentsia is done by the sedition-hunting Vigilantes, and by the saving remnant of older liberals. It is true, Dewey calls for a more attentive formulation of war-purposes and ideas, but he calls largely to deaf ears. His disciples have learned all too literally the instrumental attitude toward life, and, being immensely intelligent and energetic, they are making themselves efficient instruments of the war-technique, accepting with little question the ends as announced from above. That those ends are largely negative does not concern them, because they have never learned not to subordinate idea to technique. Their education has not given them a coherent system of large ideas, or a feeling for democratic goals. They have, in short, no clear philosophy of life except that of intelligent service, the admirable adaptation of means to ends. They are vague as to what kind of a society they want, or what kind of society America needs, but they are equipped with all the administrative attitudes and talents necessary to attain it.

To those of us who have taken Dewey's philosophy almost as our American religion, it never occurred that values could be subordinated to technique. We were instrumentalists, but we had our private utopias so clearly before our minds that the means fell always into its place as contributory. And Dewey, of course, always meant his philosophy, when taken as a philosophy of life, to start with values. But there was always that unhappy ambiguity in his doctrine as to just how values were created, and it became easier and easier to assume that just any growth was justified and almost any activity valuable so long as it achieved ends. The American, in living out this philosophy, has habitually confused results with product, and been content with getting somewhere without asking too closely whether it was the desirable place to get. It is now becoming plain that unless you start with the vividest kind of poetic vision, your instrumentalism is likely to land you just where it has landed this younger intelligentsia which is so happily and busily engaged in the national enterprise of war. You must have your vision and you must have your technique. The practical effect of Dewey's philosophy has evidently been to develop the sense of the latter at the expense of the former. Though he himself would develop them together, even in him there seems to be a flagging of values, under the influence of war. *The New Republic* honorably clamors for the Allies to subordinate military strategy to political ends, technique to democratic values. But war always undermines values. It is the outstanding lesson of the whole war that statesmen cannot be trusted to get this perspective right, that their only motto is, first to win and then grab what they can. The struggle against this statesmanlike animus must be a losing one as long as we have not very clear and very determined and very revolutionary democratic ideas and programmes to challenge them with. The trouble with our situation is not only that values have been generally ignored in favor of technique, but that those who have struggled to keep values foremost, have been too bloodless and too near-sighted in their vision. The defect of any philosophy of "adaptation" or "adjustment," even when it means adjustment to changing, living experience, is that there is no provision for thought or experience getting beyond itself. If your ideal is to be adjustment to your situation, in radiant co-operation with reality, then your success is likely to be just that and no more. You never transcend anything. You grow, but your spirit never jumps out of your skin to go on wild adventures. If your policy as a publicist reformer is to take what you can get, you are likely to find that you get something less than you should be willing to take. Italy in the settlement is said to be demanding one hundred in order to get twenty, and this machiavellian principle might well be adopted by the radical. Vision must constantly outshoot technique, opportunist efforts usually achieve less even than what seemed obviously possible. An impossibilist élan that appeals to desire will often carry further. A philosophy of adjustment will not even make for adjustment. If you try merely to "meet" situations as they come, you will not even meet them. Instead you will only pile up behind you deficits and arrears that will some day bankrupt you.

We are in the war because an American Government practised a philosophy of adjustment, and an instrumentalism for minor ends, instead of creating new values and setting at once a large standard to which the nations might repair. An intellectual attitude of mere adjustment, of mere use of the creative intelligence to make your progress, must end in caution, regression, and a virtual failure to effect even that change which you so clear-sightedly and desirously see. This is the root of our dissatisfaction with much of the current political and social realism that is preached to us. It has everything good and wise except the obstreperous vision that would drive and draw all men into it.

IV

The working-out of this American philosophy in our intellectual life then has meant an exaggerated emphasis on the mechanics of life at the expense of the quality of living. We suffer from a real shortage of spiritual values. A philosophy that worked when we were trying to get that material foundation for American life in which more impassioned living could flourish no longer works when we are faced with inexorable disaster and the hysterias of the mob. The note of complacency which we detect in the current expressions of this philosophy has a bad taste. The congruous note for the situation would seem to be, on the contrary, that of robust desperation,—a desperation that shall rage and struggle until new values come out of the travail, and we see some glimmering of our democratic way. In the creation of these new values, we may expect the old philosophy, the old radicalism, to be helpless. It has found a perfectly definite level, and there is no reason to think that it will not remain there. Its flowering appears in the technical organization of the war by an earnest group of young liberals, who direct their course by an opportunist programme of State-socialism at home and a league of benevolently-imperialistic nations abroad. At their best they can give us a government by prudent, enlightened college men instead of by politicians. At their best, they can abolish war by making everybody a partner in the booty of exploitation. That is all, and it is technically admirable. Only there is nothing in the outlook that touches in any way the happiness of the individual, the vivifying of the personality, the comprehension of social forces, the flair of art,—in other words, the quality of life. Our intellectuals have failed us as value-creators, even as value-emphasizers. The allure of the martial in war has passed only to be succeeded by the allure of the technical. The allure of fresh and true ideas, of free speculation, of artistic vigor, of cultural styles, of intelligence suffused by feeling, and feeling given fibre and outline by intelligence, has not come, and can hardly come, we see now, while our reigning philosophy is an instrumental one.

Whence can come this allure? Only from those who are thorough malcontents. Irritation at things as they are, disgust at the continual frustrations and aridities of American life, deep dissatisfaction with self and with the groups that give themselves forth as hopeful—out of such moods there might be hammered new values. The malcontents would be men and women who could not stomach the war, or the reactionary idealism that has followed in its train. They are quite through with the professional critics and classicists who have let cultural values die through their own personal ineptitude. Yet these malcontents have no intention of being cultural vandals, only to slay. They are not barbarians, but seek the vital and the sincere everywhere. All they want is a new orientation of the spirit that shall be modern, an orientation to accompany that technical orientation which is fast coming, and which the war accelerates. They will be harsh and often bad-tempered, and they will feel that the break-up of things is no time for mellowness. They will have a taste for spiritual adventure, and for sinister imaginative excursions. It will not be Puritanism so much as complacency that they will fight. A tang, a bitterness, an intellectual fibre, a verve, they will look for in literature, and their most virulent enemies will be those unaccountable radicals who are still morally servile, and are now trying to suppress all free speculation in the interests of nationalism. Something more mocking, more irreverent, they will constantly want. They will take institutions very lightly, indeed will never fail to be surprised at the seriousness with which good radicals take the stated offices and systems. Their own contempt will be scarcely veiled, and they will be glad if they can tease, provoke, irritate thought on any subject. These malcontents will be more or less of the American tribe of talent who used either to go immediately to Europe, or starved submissively at home. But these people will neither go to Europe, nor starve submissively. They are too much entangled emotionally in the possibilities of American life to leave it, and they have no desire whatever to starve. So they are likely to go ahead beating their heads at the wall until they are either bloody or light appears. They will give offense to their elders who cannot see what all the concern is about, and they will hurt the more middle-aged sense of adventure upon which the better integrated minds of the younger generation will have compromised. Optimism is often compensatory, and the optimistic mood in American thought may mean merely that American life is too terrible to face. A more skeptical, malicious, desperate, ironical mood may actually be the sign of more vivid and more stirring life fermenting in America today. It may be a sign of hope. That thirst for more of the intellectual "war and laughter" that we find Nietzsche calling us to may bring us satisfactions that optimism-haunted philosophies could never bring. Malcontentedness may be the beginning of promise. That is why I evoked the spirit of William James, with its gay passion for ideas, and its freedom of speculation, when I felt the slightly pedestrian gait into which the war had brought pragmatism. It is the creative desire more than the creative intelligence that we shall need if we are ever to fly.

9 / FREEDOM FROM TRADITION

*As a young man Van Wyck Brooks was a crusading critic
inspired with a zeal to change the whole texture of life
in America by making it hospitable to writers and
artists. Born in Plainfield, New Jersey, in 1886, he took his
bachelor's degree at Harvard in 1908, and left for
England that year, believing, as many young American
writers did, that in order to succeed an author had to
leave the United States. In England he published* The
Wine of Puritans *(1908), an essay in criticism which
emphasized two themes: the need for a usable past and
the writer's need for native roots. Brooks realized he
could not change the texture of American life, but he
could do something to change the conception of the
writer in America and the writer's conception of his own
task—in this he was to a large degree successful. In
1915 he published an influential essay,* America's Coming
of Age, *which was a denunciation of the genteel tradition
in American life and letters. In the early twenties,
he began writing impassioned essays criticizing American
authors, each essay with a moral: his work on Henry
James, the writer and expatriate, warned against the
dangers of losing touch with the people; in* The Ordeal
of Mark Twain *he attempted to demonstrate how the
author, who stayed home, was crippled by yielding to
native conventions. After 1926, Brooks began his long
career as historian of American literature, extolling the
virtues of early American writers who had been largely
neglected or held in contempt by American universities
and critical tradition.*

SOURCE: Van Wyck Brooks, "On Creating a Usable Past," from *The Dial*
LXIV (April 11, 1918), 337-41. Reprinted by permission of E. P. Dutton &
Co., Inc.

There is a kind of anarchy that fosters growth and there is another anarchy that prevents growth, because it lays too great a strain upon the individual—and all our contemporary literature in America cries out of this latter kind of anarchy. Now, anarchy is never the sheer wantonness of mind that academic people so often think it; it results from the sudden unbottling of elements that have had no opportunity to develop freely in the open; it signifies, among other things, the lack of any sense of inherited resources. English and French writers, European writers in general, never quite separate themselves from the family tree that nourishes and sustains them and assures their growth. Would American writers have done so, plainly against their best interests, if they had had any choice in the matter? I doubt it, and that is why it seems to me significant that our professors continue to pour out a stream of historical works repeating the same points of view to such an astonishing degree that they have placed a sort of Talmudic seal upon the American tradition. I suspect that the past experience of our people is not so much without elements that might be made to contribute to some common understanding in the present, as that the interpreters of that past experience have put a gloss upon it which renders it sterile for the living mind.

I am aware, of course, that we have had no cumulative culture, and that consequently the professors who guard the past and the writers who voice the present inevitably have less in common in this country than anywhere in the Old World. The professors of American literature can, after all, offer very little to the creators of it. But there is a vendetta between the two generations, and the older generation seems to delight in cutting off the supplies of the younger. What actuates the old guard in our criticism and their energetic following in the university world is apparently no sort of desire to fertilize the present, but rather to shame the present with the example of the past. There is in their note an almost pathological vindictiveness when they compare the "poetasters of today" with certain august figures of the age of pioneering who have long since fallen into oblivion in the minds of men and women of the world. Almost pathological, I say, their vindictiveness appears to be; but why not actually so? I think it is; and therefore it seems to me important, as a preliminary step to the reinterpretation of our literature, that we should have the reinterpretation of our professors that now goes merrily forward.

For the spiritual past has no objective reality; it yields only what we are able to look for in it. And what people find in literature corresponds precisely with what they find in life. Now it is obvious that professors who accommodate themselves without effort to an academic world based like ours upon the exigencies of the commercial mind cannot see anything in the past that conflicts with a commercial philosophy. Thanks to his training and environment and the typically non-creative habit of his mind, the American professor by instinct interprets his whole field of learning with reference to the ideal not of the creative, but of the practical life. He does this very often by default, but not less conclusively for that. The teaching of literature stimulates the creative faculty but it also and far more effectually thwarts it, so that the professor turns against himself. He passively plays into the hands that underfeed his own imaginative life and permits the whole weight of his meticulous knowledge of the past to tip the beam against the living present. He gradually comes to fulfill himself in the vicarious world of the dead and returns to the actual world of struggling and mis-educated mortals in the majestic raiment of borrowed immortalities. And he pours out upon that world his own contempt for the starveling poet in himself. That is why the histories of our literature so often end with a deprecating gesture at about the year 1890, why they stumble and hesitate when they discuss Whitman, why they disparage almost everything that comes out of the contemporary mind.

Now it is this that differentiates the accepted canon of American literature from those of the literatures of Europe, and invalidates it. The European professor is relatively free from these inhibitions; he views the past through the spectacles of his own intellectual freedom; consequently the corpus of inherited experience which he lays before the practicing author is not only infinitely richer and more inspiring than ours, but also more usable. The European writer, whatever his personal education may be, has his racial past, in the first place, and then he has his racial past *made available* for him. The American writer, on the other hand, not only has the most meager of birthrights but is cheated out of that. For the professorial mind, as I have said, puts a gloss upon the past that renders it sterile for the living mind. Instead of reflecting the creative impulse in American history, it reaffirms the values established by the commercial tradition; it crowns everything that has passed the censorship of the commercial and moralistic mind. And it appears to be justified because, on the whole, only those American writers who have passed that censorship have undergone a reasonably complete development and in this way entered what is often considered the purview of literary criticism.

What kind of literature it is that has passed that censorship and "succeeded" in this bustling commercial democracy of ours, we all know very well. It has been chiefly a literature of exploitation, the counterpart of our American life. From Irving and Longfellow and Cooper and Bryant, who exploited the legendary and scenic environment of our grandfathers, through the local colorists, who dominated our fiction during the intermediate age and to whom the American people accounted for artistic righteousness their own provincial quaintnesses, down to such living authors, congenial to the academic mind, as Winston Churchill, who exploits one after another the "problems" of modern society, the literature that has been allowed to live in this country, that has been imaginatively nourished, has been not only a literature acceptable to the mind that is bent upon turning the tangible world to account but a literature produced by a cognate process. Emerson, Thoreau, Whitman —there you have the exceptions, the *successful* exceptions; but they have survived not because of what they still offer us, but because they were hybrids, with enough pioneer instinct to pay their way among their contemporaries.

There is nothing to resent in this; it has been a plain matter of historic destiny. And historically predestined also is the professorial mind of today. But so is the revolt of the younger generation against the professorial mind. Aside from any personal considerations, we have the clearest sort of evidence that exploitation is alien to the true method of literature, if only because it produces the most lamentable effect on the exploiter. Look at the local colorists! They have all come to a bad end, artistically speaking. Is it necessary to recall the later work of Bret Harte after he had squeezed the orange of California? Or the lachrymosity of Mr. James Lane Allen's ghost revisiting the Kentucky apple tree from which he shook down all the fruit a generation ago? That is the sort of spectacle you have to accept complacently if you take the word of the professors that the American tradition in literature is sound and true; and the public in general does accept it complacently, because it is not averse to lachrymosity and cares nothing about the ethics of personal growth. But the conscientious writer turns aside in disgust. Seeing nothing in the past but an oblivion of all things that have meaning to the creative mood, he decides to paddle his own course, even if it leads to shipwreck.

Unhappily, the spiritual welfare of this country depends altogether upon the fate of its creative minds. If they cannot grow and ripen, where are we going to get the new ideals, the finer attitudes, that we must get if we are ever to emerge from our existing travesty of a civilization? From this point of view our contemporary literature could hardly be in a graver state. We want bold ideas, and we have nuances. We want courage, and we have universal fear. We want individuality, and we have idiosyncrasy. We want vitality, and we have intellectualism. We want emblems of desire, and we have Niagaras of emotionality. We want expansion of soul, and we have an elephantiasis of the vocal organs. Why? Because we have no cultural economy, no abiding sense of spiritual values, no body of critical understanding? Of course; that is the burden of all our criticism. But these conditions result largely, I think, from another condition that is, in part at least, remediable. The present is a void, and the American writer floats in that void because the past that survives in the common mind of the present is a past without living value. But is this the only possible past? If we need another past so badly, is it inconceivable that we might discover one, that we might even invent one?

Discover, invent a usable past we certainly can, and that is what a vital criticism always does. The past that Carlyle put together for England would never have existed if Carlyle had been an American professor. And what about the past that Michelet, groping about in the depths of his own temperament, picked out for the France of his generation? We have had our historians, too, and they have held over the dark backward of time the divining-rods of their imagination and conjured out of it what they wanted and what their contemporaries wanted—Motley's great epic of the self-made man, for instance, which he called "The Rise of the Dutch Republic." The past is an inexhaustible storehouse of apt attitudes and adaptable ideals; it opens of itself at the touch of desire; it yields up, now this treasure, now that, to anyone who comes to it armed with a capacity for personal choices. If, then, we cannot use the past our professors offer us, is there any reason why we should not create others of our own? The grey conventional mind casts its shadow backward. But why should not the creative mind dispel that shadow with shafts of light?

So far as our literature is concerned, the slightest acquaintance with other national points of view than our own is enough to show how many conceptions of it are not only possible but already exist as commonplaces in the mind of the world. Every people selects from the experience of every other people whatever contributes most vitally to its own development. The history of France that survives in the mind of Italy is totally different from the history of France that survives in the mind of England, and from this point of view there are just as many histories of America as there are nations to possess them. Go to England and you will discover that in English eyes "American literature" has become, while quite as complete an entity as it is with us, an altogether different one. You will find that an entire scheme of ideas and tendencies has survived there out of the American past to which the American academic point of view is wholly irrelevant. This, I say, is a commonplace to anyone whose mind has wandered even the shortest way from home, and to travel in one's imagination from country to country, from decade to decade, is to have this experience indefinitely multiplied. Englishmen will ask you why we Americans have so neglected Herman Melville that there is no biography of him. Russians will tell you that we never really understood the temperament of Jack London. And so on and so on, through all the ramifications of national psychology. By which I do not mean at all that we ought to cut our cloth to fit other people. I mean simply that we have every precedent for cutting it to fit ourselves. Presumably the orthodox interpreters of our literature imagine that they speak for the common reason of humankind. But evidently as regards modern literature that common reason is a very subtle and precarious thing, by no means in the possession of minds that consider it a moral duty to impose upon the world notions that have long since lost their sap. The world is far too rich to tolerate this. When Matthew Arnold once objected to Sainte-Beuve that he did not consider Lamartine an important writer, Sainte-Beuve replied, "Perhaps not, but he is important *for us.*" Only by the exercise of a little pragmatism of that kind, I think, can the past experience of our people be placed at the service of the future.

What is important for us? What, out of all the multifarious achievements and impulses and desires of the American literary mind, ought we to elect to remember? The more personally we answer this question, it seems to me, the more likely we are to get a vital order out of the anarchy of the present. For the impersonal way of answering it has been at least in part responsible for this anarchy, by severing the warm artery that ought to lead from the present back into the past. To approach our literature from the point of view not of the successful fact but of the creative impulse, is to throw it into an entirely new focus. What emerges then is the desire, the aspiration, the struggle, the tentative endeavor, and the appalling obstacles our life has placed before them. Which immediately casts over the spiritual history of America a significance that, for us, it has never had before.

Now it is impossible to make this approach without having some poignant experience of the shortcomings, the needs, and the difficulties of our literary life as it is now conditioned. Its anarchy is merely a compound of these, all of which are to be explained not so much by the absence of a cultural past as by the presence of a practical one. In particular, as I have said, this anarchy results from the sudden unbottling of elements that have had no opportunity to develop freely in the open. Why not trace those elements back, analyzing them on the way, and showing how they first manifested themselves, and why, and what repelled them? How many of Theodore Dreiser's defects, for example, are due to an environment that failed to produce the naturalistic mind until the rest of the world had outgrown it and given birth to a more advanced set of needs? And there is Vachel Lindsay. If he runs to sound and color in excess and for their sake voids himself within, how much is that because the life of a Middle Western town sets upon those things an altogether scandalous premium? Well, there you have two of the notorious difficulties of contemporary authorship; and for all that our successful tradition may say, difficulties like those have been the death of our creative life in the past. The point for us is that they have never prevented the creative impulse from being born. Look back and you will see, drifting in and out of the books of history, appearing and vanishing in the memoirs of more aggressive and more acceptable minds, all manner of queer geniuses, wraith-like personalities that have left behind them sometimes a fragment or so that has meaning for us now, more often a mere eccentric name. The creative past of this country is a limbo of the non-elect, the fathers and grandfathers of the talent of today. If they had had a little of the sun and rain that fell so abundantly upon the Goliaths of nineteenth-century philistinism, how much better conditioned would their descendants be!

The real task for the American literary historian, then, is not to seek for masterpieces—the few masterpieces are all too obvious— but for tendencies. Why did Ambrose Bierce go wrong? Why did Stephen Crane fail to acclimatize the modern method in American fiction twenty years ago? What became of Herman Melville? How did it happen that a mind capable of writing "The Story of a Country Town" should have turned up thirty years later with a book like "Success Easier Than Failure"? If we were able to answer the hundred and one questions of this sort that present themselves to every curious mind, we might throw an entirely new face not only over the past but over the present and the future also. Knowing that others have desired the things we desire and have encountered the same obstacles, and that in some degree time has begun to face those obstacles down and make the way straight for us, would not the creative forces of this country lose a little of the hectic individualism that keeps them from uniting against their common enemies? And would this not bring about, for the first time, that sense of brotherhood in effort and in aspiration which is the best promise of a national culture?

10 / FREEDOM FROM ILLUSIONS

*Joseph Wood Krutch was born in Knoxville, Tennessee,
in 1893, graduated from the University of Tennessee in
1915, and took his Ph.D. from Columbia University in
1923. He taught in the English Department at Columbia
for many years. Before his teaching career he served
in various positions on the editorial staff of* The
Nation *and was best known in his capacity of drama
critic. Toward the end of the decade of the twenties,
Krutch attempted to describe and account for the mood of
his generation, which he recognized in himself, and
which seemed to him to be reflected in contemporary
literature. He says, "My subject is not any series of
objective facts, but a state of mind, and in the effort
to describe and account for it I am responsible not for
Truth, but for the convictions, scientific or otherwise,
which I and my contemporaries have been led to
hold." His effort was to clear the air of "ghosts
from a dead world."*

Time was when the scientist, the poet, and the philosopher walked
hand in hand. In the universe which the one perceived the other
found himself comfortably at home. But the world of modern
science is one in which the intellect alone can rejoice. The mind
leaps, and leaps perhaps with a sort of elation, through the im-
mensities of space, but the spirit, frightened and cold, longs to have
once more above its head the inverted bowl beyond which may
lie whatever paradise its desires may create. The lover who sur-
rendered himself to the Implacable Aphrodite or who fancied his
foot upon the lowest rung of the Platonic ladder of love might

retain his self-respect, but one can neither resist nor yield grace-
fully to a carefully catalogued psychosis. A happy life is a sort of
poem, with a poem's elevation and dignity, but emotions cannot
be dignified unless they are first respected. They must seem to
correspond with, to be justified by, something in the structure of
the universe itself; but though it was the function of religion and
philosophy to hypostatize some such correspondence, to project a
humanity upon nature, or at least to conceive of a humane force
above and beyond her, science finds no justification for such a
process and is content instead to show how illusions were born.

The most ardent love of truth, the most resolute determination
to follow nature no matter to what black abyss she may lead, need
not blind one to the fact that many of the lost illusions had, to
speak the language of science, a survival value. Either individuals
or societies whose life is imbued with a cheerful certitude, whose
aims are clear, and whose sense of the essential rightness of life is
strong, live and struggle with an energy unknown to the skeptical
and the pessimistic. Whatever the limitations of their intellects as
instruments of criticism, they possess the physical and emotional
vigor which is, unlike critical intelligence, analogous to the processes of nature. They found empires and conquer wildernesses,
and they pour the excess of their energy into works of art which
the intelligence of more sophisticated peoples continues to admire
even though it has lost the faith in life which is requisite for the
building of a Chartres or the carving of a Venus de Milo. The one
was not erected to a law of nature or the other designed to celebrate
the *libido*, for each presupposed a sense of human dignity which
science nowhere supports.

Thus man seems caught in a dilemma which his intellect has
devised. Any deliberately managed return to a state of relative
ignorance, however desirable it might be argued to be, is obviously
out of the question. We cannot, as the naïve proponents of the
various religions, new and old, seem to assume, believe one thing
and forget another merely because we happen to be convinced
that it would be desirable to do so; and it is worth observing that
the new psychology, with its penetrating analysis of the influence
of desire upon belief, has so adequately warned the reason of the
tricks which the will can play upon it that it has greatly decreased
the possibility of beneficent delusion and serves to hold the mind

in a steady contemplation of that from which it would fain escape. Weak and uninstructed intelligences take refuge in the monotonous repetition of once living creeds, or are even reduced to the desperate expedient of going to sleep amid the formulae of the flabby pseudo-religions in which the modern world is so prolific. But neither of these classes affords any aid to the robust but serious mind which is searching for some terms upon which it may live.

And if we are, as by this time we should be, free from any teleological delusion, if we no longer make the unwarranted assumption that every human problem is somehow of necessity solvable, we must confess it may be that for the sort of being whom we have described no survival is possible in any form like that which his soul has now taken. He is a fantastic thing that has developed sensibilities and established values beyond the nature which gave him birth. He is of all living creatures the one to whom the earth is the least satisfactory. He has arrived at a point where he can no longer delude himself as to the extent of his predicament, and should he either become modified or disappear the earth would continue to spin and the grass to grow as it has always done. Of the thousands of living species the vast majority would be as unaware of his passing as they are unaware now of his presence, and he would go as a shadow goes. His arts, his religions, and his civilizations—these are fair and wonderful things, but they are fair and wonderful to him alone. With the extinction of his poetry would be extinguished also the only sensibility for which it has any meaning, and there would remain nothing capable of feeling a loss. Nothing would be left to label the memory of his discontent "divine," and those creatures who find in nature no lack would resume their undisputed possession of the earth.

Anthropoid in form some of them might continue to be, and possessed as well of all of the human brain that makes possible a cunning adaption to the conditions of physical life. To them nature might yield up subtler secrets than any yet penetrated; their machines might be more wonderful and their bodies more healthy than any yet known . . . .

. . . . .

As for this present unhappy time, haunted by ghosts from a dead world and not yet at home in its own, its predicament is not, to return to the comparison with which we began, unlike the predicament of the adolescent who has not yet learned to orient himself without reference to the mythology amid which his childhood was passed. He still seeks in the world of his experience for the values which he had found there, and he is aware only of a vast disharmony. But boys—most of them, at least—grow up, and the world of adult consciousness has always held a relation to myth intimate enough to make readjustment possible. The finest spirits have bridged the gulf, have carried over with them something of a child's faith, and only the coarsest have grown into something which was no more than finished animality. Today the gulf is broader, the adjustment more difficult, than ever it was before, and even the possibility of an actual human maturity is problematic. There impends for the human spirit either extinction or a readjustment more stupendous than any made before.

PART III

The Quest for Intellectual Freedom

(1930-1940)

A<small>FTER</small> the first bewilderment following the stock market crash of 1929 wore off, and as depression deepened month by month, Americans everywhere began to question their institutions, values, and assumptions. Business—indeed, capitalism itself—came in for heavy attack. Intellectuals who in the 1920's had accused the business society of being unable to fulfill the spiritual needs of man now charged that it was also incapable of meeting man's physical needs. Americans' traditional optimism wavered and their faith in inevitable progress was shaken. Many people saw the grim irony symbolized in 1932 by the Century of Progress Exposition taking place in Chicago surrounded by idle factories—this spectacle of a country proclaiming its technological achievements while 15 million of its citizens were jobless, seemed to underscore the hollowness of the doctrine of inevitable progress. Within this context, it is not surprising that relativism was used to topple the last remaining supports of the old order in an attempt to establish complete intellectual freedom to plan a new world.

It is true that the early proponents of pragmatism, instrumentalism, and naturalism, by accepting the findings of science, particularly Darwinian evolution, had apparently established the proposition that all truths were relative. They maintained that the universe was plastic, and that the only way man could adjust to the process of continuous flux and change was through the rational application of the findings of science. They assumed that trained experts, scientists, could discover and organize sufficient data about objective reality to show the way for man to adapt comfortably to changed conditions. Progressives, if they did nothing else, popularized the cult of science and established the authority of experts. They insisted on the necessity of acting on the basis of a thorough knowledge of facts, establishing innumerable fact-finding commissions and legislative reference libraries to facilitate their accumulation. But the implication was that the facts, once established, would show the one right way to a better world. Every field in the natural and social sciences was dominated by conservative expert-scholars who lent support to the status quo. Many of these men insisted that they had arrived at their position through an expert and objective reading of the facts. So, in order to break free of the restraints of such experts, the relativists sought to undermine their authority. Percy Bridgeman, a physicist, applied the implications of his studies in quantum mechanics to philosophy and social thought (Selection 11), Carl Becker and Charles Beard developed the philosophic implications of relativism in their historical studies (Selections 12 and 14), and Jerome Frank developed a relativistic approach to the science of law known as *legal realism* (Selection 13).

The relativism implicit in evolutionary and pragmatic thought insisted only that everything was undergoing change, but did not question man's ability to determine the nature, direction, and rate of change. The new relativists, inspired by Einstein's theory of relativity and Freudian psychology, questioned man's ability to make any objective determinations that would be true for any time or place. As early as 1921, a critic in the *London Times Literary Supplement* declared that

. . . the theory of relativity, promises to develop into a principle as adequate to universal application as the theory of evolution. This latter theory, from being a technical biological hypothesis, became an inspiring guide to workers in practically every branch of knowledge: manners and customs, morals, religions, philosophies, arts, steam engines, electric tramways—everything had "evolved." . . . We are hardy enough to prophesy a similar career and fate for the theory of relativity. The technical physical theory, at present imperfectly understood, will become still more vague and dim. History repeats itself, and relativity, like evolution, after receiving a number of intelligible but somewhat inaccurate popular expositions in its scientific aspect, will be launched in a world conquering career. We suggest that, by that time, it will probably be called *Relativismus*. Many of these larger applications will doubtless be justified; some will be absurd and a considerable number will, we imagine, reduce to truisms. And the physical theory, the mere seed of this mighty growth, will become once more the purely technical concern of scientific men.

By 1941 the prophecy seemed to be realized. As Esmond Wright declared,

Darwin's star has waned before the flood of new biological and scientific research. The new watchword is the relativity of all abstract schemes to the conditions of the age in which they are produced.

11 / THE REVOLUTION IN PHYSICS

P. W. Bridgeman is a physicist who extended his research analysis to the problems of philosophy. He was born in 1882 in Cambridge, Massachusetts, and educated at Harvard, where he secured his Ph.D. in 1908 and became a member of the physics department. In 1926 he was made Hollis Professor of Mathematics and Natural Philosophy, and in 1946 he was awarded the Nobel Prize in physics for his studies of atmospheric pressure. In a very influential book, The Logic of Modern Physics (1927), Bridgeman first stated extensively his concept of operationalism, a method for resolving social problems and eliminating meaningless disputes that have been the result of vague terminology by clarifying significant differences where they exist. In this selection, Bridgeman makes clear the development of relativism and quantum mechanics and tries to assess their implications for social thought.

The attitude which the man in the street unconsciously adopts toward science is capricious and varied. At one moment he scorns the

SOURCE: Percy W. Bridgeman, "The New Vision of Science" in *Reflections of a Physicist*, 2d ed. (New York: Philosophical Library, 1955), pp. 167-89.

scientist for a highbrow, at another anathematizes him for blasphemously undermining his religion; but at the mention of a name like Edison he falls into a coma of veneration. When he stops to think, he does recognize, however, that the whole atmosphere of the world in which he lives is tinged by science, as is shown most immediately and strikingly by our modern conveniences and material resources. A little deeper thinking shows him that the influence of science goes much farther and colors the entire mental outlook of modern civilized man on the world about him. Perhaps one of the most telling evidences of this is his growing freedom from superstition. Freedom from superstition is the result of the conviction that the world is not governed by caprice, but that it is a world of order and can be understood by man if he will only try hard enough and be clever enough. This conviction that the world is understandable is, doubtless, the most important single gift of science to civilization. The widespread acceptance of this view can be dated to the discovery by Newton of the universal sway of the law of gravitation; and for this reason Newton may be justly regarded as the most important single contributor to modern life.

The point of view for which Newton is responsible is well exemplified by the remark often made that every particle of matter in the universe attracts to some extent every other particle, even though the attraction is almost inconceivably minute. There is thus presented to the mind a sublime picture of the interrelatedness of all things; all things are subject to law, and the universe is in this respect a unit. As a corollary to this conviction about the structure of the universe, an equally important conviction as to man's place in the universe has been growing up; man feels more and more that he is in a congenial universe, that he is part and parcel of everything around him, that the same laws that make things outside him go also make him go, and that, therefore, he can, by taking sufficient pains, understand these laws. These two theses so closely related—that the world is a world of order and that man can find the guiding motif of this order—have come to be the tacit cardinal articles of faith of the man of science, and from him have diffused through the entire social structure, so that now some such conviction essentially colors the thinking of every educated person. It is to be emphasized that the justification for this conviction is entirely in experience; it is true that, as man has grown older and acquired more extensive acquaintance with nature and pondered more deeply, he has been increasingly successful in reducing the world about him to order and understandability. It has been most natural to generalize this experience into the conviction that this sort of thing will always be possible, and to believe that as we delve constantly deeper we shall always be able to give a rational account of what we find, although very probably the difficulties will become continually greater.

The thesis of this article is that the age of Newton is now coming to a close, and that recent scientific discoveries have in store an even greater revolution in our entire outlook than the revolution effected by the discovery of universal gravitation by Newton. The revolution that now confronts us arises from the recent discovery of new facts, the only interpretation of which is that our conviction that nature is understandable and subject to law arose from the narrowness of our horizons, and that if we sufficiently extend our range we shall find that nature is intrinsically and in its elements neither understandable nor subject to law.

The task of the rest of this article is twofold. In the first place I shall try to give some suggestion of the nature of the physical evidence and of the reasoning that has forced the physicist to the conclusion that nature is constituted in this way. This task is by no means easy; for not only is it impossible to indicate more than very partially the physical evidence, but it is often necessary to compress into a few sentences steps in the reasoning that can be completely justified only by long and difficult mathematical or logical analysis. The second part of the task is to envisage a few of the far-reaching consequences on the whole outlook of mankind of the acceptance of the view that this is actually the structure of nature. This aspect of the situation can be appreciated without a detailed grasp of the preliminary analysis.

II

The new experimental facts are in the realm of quantum phenomena. Comparatively little has been written for popular consumption about this new realm which has opened in the last fifteen years. The man in the street has been much more interested in relativity, which to him has seemed extremely interesting and revolutionary. Occasionally, however, there has filtered down to him the news that nearly all the theoretical physicists are occupied with a new order of phenomena which they find very much more exciting and revolutionary than any in the realm of relativity. For after all is said and done, the practical effects of relativity, measured in dollars and cents or in centimeters and grams, are exceedingly small, and require specially designed experiments executed by men of the highest skill to show their existence at all. The phenomena with which quantum theory deals, on the other hand, are of the greatest practical importance and involve the simplest aspects of everyday life. For example, before the advent of quantum theory no one could explain why a tea kettle of water boiling on the stove should not give out enough light in virtue of its temperature to be visible in the dark; the accepted theories of optics demanded that it should be visible, but every burned child knew that it was not.

One reason that the man in the street has not sensed this new domain is that it is much more difficult to explain than relativity; this is partly due to the nature of the subject, and partly also to the fact that the physicist himself does not understand the subject as well. I shall not in this article rush in where the angels have not ventured, but it is, nevertheless, necessary to try to give a glimmering of an idea of what it is all about.

Although all the phenomena of ordinary life are really quantum phenomena, they do not begin to stand out unequivocally in their quantum aspect and admit of no other interpretation until we have penetrated very far down into the realm of small things and have arrived at the atoms and electrons themselves. It must not be pretended that the nature of the quantum phenomena met in this realm of small things is by any means completely understood; but a suggestive characterization of the general situation is that atomicity or discontinuity is an even more pervading characteristic of the structure of the universe than had been previously supposed. In fact the name, "quantum," was suggested by the atomicity.

We were a long time in convincing ourselves of the atomic structure of ordinary matter; although this was guessed by the poets as early as the beginning of the Christian era, it was not generally accepted as proved, even by physicists, until the beginning of this century. The next step was the discovery of the atomic structure of electricity; there are indivisible units of positive and negative electricity, and the atoms of matter are constructed of atoms of electricity. This situation was not even guessed until about 1890; the proof and acceptance of the doctrine have taken place within the memory of the majority of the readers of this article. Finally comes the discovery that, not only is matter doubly atomic in its structure, but that there is an atomicity in the way in which one piece of matter acts on another. This is perhaps best understood in the case of optical phenomena. It used to be thought that light was infinitely subdivisible—that I could, for example, receive at pleasure on the film of my camera either the full intensity of the sun's radiation, or, by interposing a sufficiently small stop, that I could cut the intensity of the light down to anything this side of nothing at all. This is now known not to be true; but the light which we receive from the sun is atomic in structure, like an almost inconceivably fine rain composed of indivisible individual drops, rather than like the continuous flood of infinitely subdivisible radiation that we had supposed. If I close the stop of my camera too much I may receive nothing at all on the film, or I may receive a single one of the drops in the rain of radiation, but there is no step between one drop and nothing. The recognition that radiation has this property means that in some respects we have come back very close to Newton's ideas about light.

The proof that this is the structure of light can be given in many ways. Perhaps the most illuminating for our purpose is that discovered by Arthur Compton, for which he received the Nobel prize. Compton's discovery consisted in finding that the drops of radiation behave in certain ways like the material drops of ordinary rain; they have energy and mass and momentum, which means that when they collide with matter they behave in some respects very much as ordinary bodies do. The laws which govern the interaction or collision of ordinary bodies are known to any graduate of a high-school course in physics; he could calculate what would happen after two billiard balls had collided provided we would tell him exactly how each of the balls was moving before the collision, and what were the elastic properties of the materials of which the balls are composed. In making the calculation he would use, among other things, the two fundamental principles of the conservation of energy and the conservation of momentum. Now Compton showed that what happens when a drop, or better a bullet, of radiation collides with an electron is also governed by the same two fundamental principles. The proof consisted in showing that the way in which the electron rebounds is connected with the way in which the bullet rebounds by equations deduced from these principles; this is one of the features which makes Compton's discovery of such a fundamental importance.

But Compton's experiment contains another feature, and it is this which seems destined to revolutionize the thinking of civilization. Go back to the billiard-ball analogy: An expert billiard player can, by proper manipulation of the cue ball, make the two balls rebound from the collision as he wishes; this involves the ability to predict how the balls will move after collision from their behavior before collision. We should expect by analogy to be able to do the same thing for a collision between a bullet of radiation and an electron; but the fact is that it never has been done and, if our present theories are correct, in the nature of things never can be done. It is true that, if someone will tell me how the electron bounces away, I can tell, on the basis of the equations given by Compton's theory, how the bullet of radiation bounces away, or conversely; but no one has ever been able to tell how both will bounce away. Billiards, played with balls like this, even by a player of infinite skill, would degenerate into a game of pure chance.

This unpredictable feature has been seized and incorporated as one of the cornerstones in the new theory of quantum mechanics, which has so stirred the world of physicists in the last three years. It has received implicit formulation in the "Principle of Uncertainty" of Heisenberg, a principle which I believe is fraught with the possibility of greater change in mental outlook than was ever packed into an equal number of words. The exact formulation of the principle, which is very brief, is framed in too technical language to reproduce here, but I shall try to give the spirit of the principle. The essence of it is that there are certain inherent limitations to the accuracy with which a physical situation can be described. Of course we have always recognized that all our physical measurements are necessarily subject to error; but it has always been thought that, if we took pains enough and were sufficiently clever, no bounds could be set to the accuracy which we might some day achieve. Heisenberg's principle states, on the other hand, that the ultimately possible accuracy of our measurements is limited in a curious and unsuspected way. There is no limit to the accuracy with which we can describe (or measure) any one quality in a physical situation, but if we elect to measure one thing accurately we pay a price in our inability to measure some other thing accurately. Specifically, in Compton's experiment, the principle states that we can measure the position of the electron as accurately as we choose, but in so doing we must sacrifice by a compensating amount the possibility of accurately measuring its velocity. In particular, if we measure with perfect accuracy the position of the electron, we have thereby denied ourselves the possibility of making any measurement at all of its velocity.

The meaning of the fact that it is impossible to measure exactly both the position and velocity of the electron may be paradoxically stated to be that an electron cannot have both position and velocity. The justification of this is to be found in the logical analysis of the meaning of our physical concepts which has been stimulated by the relativity theory of Einstein. On careful examination the physicist finds that in the sense in which he uses language no meaning at all can be attached to a physical concept which cannot ultimately be described in terms of some sort of measurement. A body has position only in so far as its position can be measured; if its position cannot in principle be measured, the concept of position applied to the body is meaningless, or in other words, a position of the body does not exist. Hence if both the position and velocity of the electron cannot in principle be measured, the electron cannot have both position and velocity; position and velocity as expressions of properties which an electron can simultaneously have are meaningless. To carry the paradox one step farther, by choosing whether I shall measure the position or velocity of the electron I thereby determine whether the electron has position or velocity. The physical properties of the electron are not absolutely inherent in it, but involve also the choice of the observer.

Return to the analogy of the billiard ball. If we ask our high-school physicist what he must be told before he can predict how the billiard balls will rebound after collision, he will say that, unless he is told both how fast the balls are traveling when they collide, and also what their relative positions are at the moment of collision he can do very little. But this is exactly the sort of thing that the Heisenberg principle says no one can ever tell; so that our high-school computer would never be able to predict how a bullet of radiation and an electron behave after collision, and no more could we. This means that in general when we get down to fine-scale phenomena the detailed results of interaction between the individual elements of which our physical world are composed are essentially unpredictable.

This principle has been built into a theory, and the theory has been checked in many ways against experiment, and always with complete success. One of the consequences of which the man in the street has heard a good deal is that an electron has some of the properties of waves, as shown so strikingly in the experiments of Davisson and Germer. Of course no one can say that some day a fact may not be discovered contrary to the principle, but up to the present there is no evidence of it; and it is certain that some-thing very much like this principle, if not this principle exactly, covers an enormously wide range of phenomena. In fact the prin-ciple probably governs every known type of action between differ-ent parts of our physical universe. One reason that this principle has not been formulated before is that the error which it tells us is inherent in all measurement is so small that only recently have methods become accurate enough to detect it. The error is unim-portant, and indeed immeasurably small when we are dealing with the things of ordinary life. The extreme minuteness of the effect can be illustrated again with the billiard balls. Suppose that at the instant of collision the position of the balls is known with an un-certainty no greater than the diameter of a single atom, a precision very much higher than has ever been attained. Then the principle says that it is impossible to measure the velocity of the balls without a related uncertainty; but on figuring it out we find that this un-certainty is so small that after the lapse of one hundred thousand years, assuming a billiard table large enough for the balls to con-tinue rolling for one hundred thousand years, the additional uncer-tainty in the position of the balls arising from the uncertainty in the velocity would again be only the diameter of a single atom. The error becomes important only when we are concerned with the ulti-mately small constituents of things, such as the action between one atom and another or between an atom of radiation and an electron.

III

It is easy to see why the discovery that nature is constituted in this way, and in particular is essentially unpredictable, has been so enormously upsetting. For the ability to predict a happening is tied up with our ideas of cause and effect. When we say that the future is causally determined by the present we mean that if we are given a complete description of the present the future is completely determined, or in other words, the future is the effect of the present, which is the cause. This causal relation is a bilateral relation; given the cause, the effect is determined, or given the effect, the cause may be deduced. But this means, in the particular case that we have been considering of collision between a bullet of radiation and an electron, that the causal connection does not exist, for if it did the way in which the electron rebounds after the collision would be determined, that is, it could be predicted, in terms of what happens before the collision. Conversely, it is of course impossible to reconstruct from the way in which the electron and the radiation rebound the way in which they were moving before collision. Hence the rebound of the electron is not causally connected with what goes before.

The same situation confronts the physicist everywhere; whenever he penetrates to the atomic or electronic level in his analysis, he finds things acting in a way for which he can assign no cause, for which he never can assign a cause, and for which the concept of cause has no meaning, if Heisenberg's principle is right. This means nothing more nor less than that the law of cause and effect must be given up. The precise reason that the law of cause and effect fails can be paradoxically stated; it is not that the future is not determined in terms of a complete description of the present, but that in the nature of things the present cannot be completely described.

The failure of the law of cause and effect has been exploited by a number of German physicists, who have emphasized the conclusion that we are thus driven to recognize that the universe is governed by pure chance; this conclusion does not, I believe, mean quite what appears on the surface, but in any event we need not trouble ourselves with the further implications of this statement, in spite of their evident interest.

One may be sure that a principle as revolutionary in its implications as this, which demands the sacrifice of what had become the cardinal article of faith of the physicist, has not been accepted easily, but there has been a great deal of pondering and searching of fundamentals.

The result of all this pondering has been to discover in the principle an inevitableness, which when once understood, is so convincing that we have already almost ceased to kick against the pricks. This inevitableness is rooted in the structure of knowledge. It is a commonplace that we can never know anything about anything without getting into some sort of connection with it, either direct or indirect. We, or someone else, must smell the object, or taste it, or touch it, or hear it, or see it, or it must affect some other object which can affect our senses either directly or indirectly, before we can know anything about it, even its existence. This means that no knowledge of any physical property or of even mere existence is possible without interaction; in fact these terms have no meaning apart from interaction. Formerly, if this aspect of the situation was thought of at all, it would have been dismissed as merely of academic interest, of no pertinence at all, and the justification of this would have been found in the supposed possibility of making the inevitable interaction as small as we pleased. The defender of the old point of view might have flippantly remarked that a cat may look at a king, by which he would have meant that the act of observation has no effect on the object. But even in the old days a captious critic might have objected to this easy self-satisfaction by pointing out that light exerts a pressure, so that light cannot pass from the king to the cat without the exercise of a certain amount of mechanical repulsion between them. This remark of the captious critic now ceases to be merely academic because of the discovery that light itself is atomic in structure, so that at least one bullet of radiation must pass if any light at all passes, and the king cannot be observed at all without the exertion of that minimum amount of mechanical repulsion which corresponds to a single bullet.

This evidently alters the entire situation. The mere act of giving meaning through observation to any physical property of a thing involves a certain minimum amount of interaction. Now if there are definite characteristics associated with the minimum interaction, it is conceivable that no observation of anything whatever can be made without entraining certain universal consequences, and this turns out to be the case. Let us return again to the useful billiard-ball analogy. What must our high-school calculator know in order completely to calculate the behavior of the balls after collision? Evidently, if he is to give a complete description of the motion, that is, give in addition to direction and velocity of motion the exact time at which the balls are in any particular location, he must know how long the collision lasts. This means that the act of collision itself must be analyzed. This analysis is actually possible, and in fact rapid-moving pictures have been taken, showing in detail how the balls are deformed during their contact together.

Returning now to the collision between a bullet of radiation and an electron, in order to determine completely the behavior after collision we must similarly analyze the details of the process of collision. In particular, if we want to predict where the electron is after collision we must analyze the collision sufficiently to be able to say how fast the electron is moving at each instant of the collision. But how shall this analysis be made? If the analysis means anything, it must involve the possibility of observation; and observation involves interaction; and interaction cannot be reduced below a minimum. But the collision, or interaction, between the electron and radiation that we are analyzing is itself the minimum interaction. It is obvious that we cannot discover fine details with an instrument as coarse as the thing that we are trying to analyze, so that the necessary analysis of the minimum interaction can never be made, and hence has no meaning, because of our fundamental dictum that things which cannot in principle be measured have no meaning. Therefore, the act of collision cannot be analyzed, the electron and radiation during collision have no measurable properties, and the ordinary concepts, which depend on these properties, do not apply during collision, and have no meaning. In particular, the ordinary concept of velocity does not apply to the act of collision, and we are prepared to expect something curious as the result of the collision. In fact, the detailed working out of the theory shows that the meaninglessness of velocity during the act of collision carries with it the consequence that the electron emerges from the collision with a certain nebulosity or indefiniteness in properties such as position, which according to the old point of view depend on the velocity, and it is precisely this nebulosity which is described in Heisenberg's principle.

The infinitesimal world thus takes on a completely new aspect, and it will doubtless be a long while before the average human mind finds a way of dealing satisfactorily with a situation so foreign to ordinary experience. Almost the first necessity is a renunciation of our present verbal habits and of their implications. It is extraordinarily difficult to deal with this new situation with our present forms of expression, and the exposition of this paper is no exception. The temptation is almost irresistible to say and to think that the electron *really* has *both* position and velocity, only the trouble is that our methods of measurement are subject to some limitation which prevents us from measuring both simultaneously. An attitude like this is justified by all the experience of the past, because we have always been able hitherto to continue to refine our methods of measurement after we had apparently reached the end. But here we are confronted by a situation which in principle contains something entirely novel, and the old expectations are no longer valid. The new situation cannot be adequately dealt with until long-continued familiarity with the new facts produces in our subconsciousness as instinctive a grasp as that which we now have of the familiar relations of everyday experience.

IV

The implications of this discovery are evidently most far-reaching. Let us first consider the scientific implications and, in particular, the implications for physics. The physicist is here brought to the end of his domain. The record of physics up to the present has been one of continued expansion, ever penetrating deeper and deeper, and always finding structure on a finer and finer scale beyond previous achievement. Several times in the past even eminent physicists have permitted themselves the complacent announcement that we were in sight of the end, and that the explanation of all things was in our hands. But such predictions have always been set at naught by the discovery of finer details, until the average physicist feels an instinctive horror of the folly of prediction. But here is a situation new and unthought of. We have reached the point where knowledge must stop because of the nature of knowledge itself: beyond this point meaning ceases.

It may seem that we are getting back pretty close to the good Bishop Berkeley, but I think that actually nothing could be wider of the mark. We are not saying that nothing exists where there is no consciousness to perceive it; we are saying that existence has meaning only when there is interaction with other existence, but direct contact with consciousness need not come until the end of a long chain. The logician will have no trouble in showing that this description of the situation is internally self-contradictory and does not make sense; but I believe that, nevertheless, the sympathetic reader will be able to see what the situation is, and will perhaps subscribe to the opinion that to describe it the development of a new language is necessary.

The physicist thus finds himself in a world from which the bottom has dropped clean out; as he penetrates deeper and deeper it eludes him and fades away by the highly unsportsmanlike device of just becoming meaningless. No refinement of measurement will avail to carry him beyond the portals of this shadowy domain which he cannot even mention without logical inconsistency. A bound is thus forever set to the curiosity of the physicist. What is more, the mere existence of this bound means that he must give up his most cherished convictions and faith. The world is not a world of reason, understandable by the intellect of man, but as we penetrate ever deeper, the very law of cause and effect, which we had thought to be a formula to which we could force God Himself to subscribe, ceases to have meaning. The world is not intrinsically reasonable or understandable; it acquires these properties in ever-increasing degree as we ascend from the realm of the very little to the realm of everyday things; here we may eventually hope for an understanding sufficiently good for all practical purposes, but no more.

The thesis that this is the structure of the world was not reached by armchair meditation, but it is the interpretation of direct experiment. Now all experiment is subject to error, and no one can say that some day new experimental facts may not be found incompatible with our present interpretation; all we can say is that at present we have no glimmering of such a situation. But whether or not the present interpretation will survive, a vision has come to the physicist in this experience which he will never forget; the possibility that the world may fade away, elude him, and become meaningless because of the nature of knowledge itself, has never been envisaged before, at least by the physicist, and this possibility must forever keep him humble.

When this view of the structure of nature has once been accepted by physicists after a sufficiently searching experimental probe, it is evident that there will be a complete revolution in the aspect of all the other physical sciences. The mental outlook will change; the mere feeling that boundaries are set to man's inquiry will produce a subtle change of attitude no less comprehensive in its effects than the feeling, engendered by Newton's conquest of celestial mechanics, that the universe was a universe of order accessible to the mind of man. The immediate effect on scientific inquiry will be to divert effort away from the more obviously physical fields back to the fields of greater complication, which have been passed over by the physicist in his progress toward the ultimately little, especially the field of biology.

Another important result of the realization of the structure of the world is that the scientist will see that his program is finite. The scientist is perhaps only a passing phase in the evolution of man; after unguessable years it is not impossible that his work will be done, and the problems of mankind will become for each individual the problem of best ordering his own life. Or it may be that the program of the scientist, although finite, will turn out to need more time than the life of the world itself.

But doubtless by far the most important effect of this revolution will not be on the scientist, but on the man in the street. The immediate effect will be to let loose a veritable intellectual spree of licentious and debauched thinking. This will come from the refusal to take at its true value the statement that it is meaningless to penetrate much deeper than the electron, and will have the thesis that there *is really* a domain beyond, only that man with his present limitations is not fitted to enter this domain. The temptation to deal with the situation in this way is one that not many who have not been trained in careful methods of thinking will be able to resist —one reason is in the structure of language. Thought has a predisposition to certain tendencies merely because of the necessity of expressing itself in words. This has already been brought out sufficiently by the discussion above; we have seen how difficult it is to express in words the fact that the universe fades away from us by becoming meaningless without the implication that there really is something beyond the verge of meaning.

The man in the street will, therefore, twist the statement that the scientist has come to the end of meaning into the statement that the scientist has penetrated as far as he can with the tools at his command, and that there is something beyond the ken of the scientist. This imagined beyond, which the scientist has proved he cannot penetrate, will become the playground of the imagination of every mystic and dreamer. The existence of such a domain will be made the basis of an orgy of rationalizing. It will be made the substance of the soul; the spirits of the dead will populate it; God will lurk in its shadows; the principle of vital processes will have its seat here; and it will be the medium of telepathic communication. One group will find in the failure of the physical law of cause and effect the solution of the age-long problem of the freedom of the will; and on the other hand the atheist will find the justification of his contention that chance rules the universe.

Doubtless generations will be needed to adjust our thinking so that it will spontaneously and freely conform to our knowledge of the actual structure of the world. It is probable that new methods of education will have to be painfully developed and applied to very young children in order to inculcate the instinctive and successful use of habits of thought so contrary to those which have been naturally acquired in meeting the limited situations of everyday life. This does not mean at all that the new methods of thought will be less well adapted than those we now have to meet the situations of everyday life, but on the contrary, since thought will conform to reality, understanding and conquest of the world about us will proceed at an accelerated pace. I venture to think that there will also eventually be a favorable effect on man's character; the mean man will react with pessimism, but a certain courageous nobility is needed to look a situation like this in the face. And in the end, when man has fully partaken of the fruit of the tree of knowledge, there will be this difference between the first Eden and the last, that man will not become as a god, but will remain forever humble.

12 / RELATIVITY AND HISTORY

*Carl Becker stands along with his teachers, Frederick
Jackson Turner and Charles Beard, as one of the most
literate and influential writers among American
historians. He was born in 1873, graduated from the
University of Wisconsin in 1896, and took his Ph.D. there
in 1907. He was a member of the history department at
the University of Kansas from 1902 to 1916, then in
1917 joined the history faculty at Cornell University,
where he served until his death in 1945.
Becker was always concerned with the nature of the
historian's task and of historical fact. He became
increasingly sceptical of the historian's ability to maintain
his objectivity or to achieve any certainty about the
past. He, along with Charles Beard, developed the
philosophic implications of relativism and instrumentalism
for historical studies. He insisted that the historian is
present-minded and that his own judgments and
values become an inextricable part of the history he
writes. His* The Heavenly City of the Eighteenth-Century
Philosophers *(1932) is a classic exposition and example
of the philosophic problems he dealt with throughout
his career. ¶In his book he attempts to analyze the
underlying assumptions of the eighteenth-century
Enlightenment and maintains that the clue to an age can
be found in concepts that serve as fundamental,
unquestioned postulates of its outlook. Such ideas are
seldom analyzed by contemporaries because they
are the tools with which all else is explained. For example,
in the eighteenth century, "nature" and "natural law"
were terms providing a common ground. In this*

SOURCE: Carl L. Becker, "Climates of Opinion," Chapter I in *The Heavenly
City of the Eighteenth-Century Philosophers* (New Haven: Yale University
Press, 1932), pp. 11-28.

*selection, Becker attempts to clear the intellectual
air of any illusion of absolute certainty implied by the
unquestioning use of particularly solid words.*

We have now remained in the medieval climate of opinion as long
as it is perhaps quite safe to do. Let us then descend from the peaks
of the thirteenth to the lower levels of the twentieth century—to
an atmosphere in which, since it is charged with a richer factual
content, we can breathe with greater ease and comfort.

II

What then can we—scientists, historians, philosophers of the twentieth century—make of the theology-history, the philosophy-science,
the dialectic-methodology of the thirteenth century? We can—must,
indeed, since that is our habit—peruse with infinite attention and
indifference the serried, weighty folios of the *Summa* and such
works now carefully preserved in libraries. We can perhaps wonder
a little—although, since nothing is alien to us, we are rarely caught
wondering—at the unfailing zest, the infinite patience, the extraordinary ingenuity and acumen therein displayed. We can even understand what is therein recorded well enough to translate it
clumsily into modern terms. The one thing we cannot do with the
Summa of St. Thomas is to meet its arguments on their own ground.
We can neither assent to them nor refute them. It does not even
occur to us to make the effort, since we instinctively feel that in
the climate of opinion which sustains such arguments we could
only gasp for breath. Its conclusions seem to us neither true nor
false, but only irrelevant; and they seem irrelevant because the
world pattern into which they are so dexterously woven is no longer
capable of eliciting from us either an emotional or an aesthetic
response.

With the best will in the world it is quite impossible for us to
conceive of existence as a divinely ordered drama, the beginning
and end of which is known, the significance of which has once for
all been revealed. For good or ill we must regard the world as a
continuous flux, a ceaseless and infinitely complicated process of
waste and repair, so that "all things and principles of things" are to

be regarded as no more than "inconstant modes or fashions," as
the "concurrence, renewed from moment to moment, of forces part-
ing sooner or later on their way." The beginning of this continuous
process of change is shrouded in impenetrable mist; the end seems
more certain, but even less engaging. According to J. H. Jeans:

Everything points with overwhelming force to a definite event, or
series of events, of creation at some time or times, not infinitely remote.
The universe cannot have originated by chance out of its present in-
gredients, and neither can it have been always the same as now. For in
either of these events no atoms would be left save such as are incapable
of dissolving into radiation; there would be neither sunlight nor starlight
but only a cool glow of radiation uniformly diffused through space. This
is, indeed, so far as present-day science can see, the final end towards
which all creation moves, and at which it must at long last arrive.[1]

We need not, of course, make immediate preparation for that
far-off, portentous event; the universe is still a going concern and
will outlast our time. But we may be reasonably curious about the
relation of man to this inevitable running down of the universe.
How did man enter this galley, and what is he doing in it? According to Professor Dampier-Whetham, science offers two possible
answers:

Life . . . may be regarded either as a negligible accident in a by-
product of the cosmic process, or as the supreme manifestation of the
high effort of creative evolution, for which the Earth alone, in the
chances of time and space, has given a fitting home.[2]

Between these alternatives there is little enough to choose, since
in either case man must be regarded as part of the cosmic process,
fated to extinction with it. Let us listen to Bertrand Russell:

That man is the product of causes which had no prevision of the end
they were achieving; that his origin, his growth, his hopes and fears,
his loves and his beliefs, are but the outcome of accidental collocations
of atoms; that no fire, no heroism, no intensity of thought and feeling
can preserve an individual life beyond the grave; that all the labours
of all the ages, all the devotion, all the inspiration, all the noonday
brightness of human genius are destined to extinction in the vast death
of the solar system, and that the whole temple of man's achievement

[1] *Eos, or the Wider Aspects of Cosmogony*, p. 55; quoted in Dampier-Whetham,
A History of Science, p. 483.   [2] *A History of Science*, p. 482.

must inevitably be buried beneath the debris of a universe in ruins—all these things, if not quite beyond dispute, are yet so nearly certain that no philosophy which rejects them can hope to stand.[3]

Edit and interpret the conclusions of modern science as tenderly as we like, it is still quite impossible for us to regard man as the child of God for whom the earth was created as a temporary habitation. Rather must we regard him as little more than a chance deposit on the surface of the world, carelessly thrown up between two ice ages by the same forces that rust iron and ripen corn, a sentient organism endowed by some happy or unhappy accident with intelligence indeed, but with an intelligence that is conditioned by the very forces that it seeks to understand and to control. The ultimate cause of this cosmic process of which man is a part, whether God or electricity or a "stress in the ether," we know not. Whatever it may be, if indeed it be anything more than a necessary postulate of thought, it appears in its effects as neither benevolent nor malevolent, as neither kind nor unkind, but merely as indifferent to us. What is man that the electron should be mindful of him! Man is but a foundling in the cosmos, abandoned by the forces that created him. Unparented, unassisted and undirected by omniscient or benevolent authority, he must fend for himself, and with the aid of his own limited intelligence find his way about in an indifferent universe.

Such is the world pattern that determines the character and direction of modern thinking. The pattern has been a long time in the weaving. It has taken eight centuries to replace the conception of existence as divinely composed and purposeful drama by the conception of existence as a blindly running flux of disintegrating energy. But there are signs that the substitution is now fully accomplished; and if we wished to reduce eight centuries of intellectual history to an epigram, we could not do better than to borrow the words of Aristophanes, "Whirl is king, having deposed Zeus."

Perhaps the most important consequence of this revolution is that we look about in vain for any semblance of the old authority, the old absolute, for any stable foothold from which to get a running start. Zeus, having been deposed, can no longer serve as a first premise of thought. It is true we may still believe in Zeus; many

[3] *Mysticism and Logic,* p. 47; quoted in Dampier-Whetham, *A History of Science,* p. 487.

people do. Even scientists, historians, philosophers still accord him
the customary worship. But this is no more than a personal privilege, to be exercised in private, as formerly, in Protestant countries,
Papists were sometimes permitted to celebrate mass in private
chapels. No serious scholar would now postulate the existence and
goodness of God as a point of departure for explaining the quantum theory or the French Revolution. If I should venture, as certain historians once did, to expound the thought of the eighteenth
century as having been foreordained by God for the punishment of
a perverse and stiff-necked generation, you would shift uneasily in
your chairs, you would "register" embarrassment, and even blush
a little to think that a trusted colleague should exhibit such bad
taste. The fact is that we have no first premise. Since Whirl is king,
we must start with the whirl, the mess of things as presented in
experience. We start with the irreducible brute fact, and we must
take it as we find it, since it is no longer permitted to coax or ca-
jole it, hoping to fit it into some or other category of thought on
the assumption that the pattern of the world is a logical one. Accepting the fact as given, we observe it, experiment with it, verify
it, classify it, measure it if possible, and reason about it as little as
may be. The questions we ask are "What?" and "How?" What are
the facts and how are they related? If sometimes, in a moment of
absent-mindedness or idle diversion, we ask the question "Why?"
the answer escapes us. Our supreme object is to measure and master the world rather than to understand it.

Since our supreme object is to measure and master the world, we
can make relatively little use of theology, philosophy, and deductive logic—the three stately entrance ways to knowledge erected
in the Middle Ages. In the course of eight centuries these disciplines have fallen from their high estate, and in their place we
have enthroned history, science, and the technique of observation
and measurement. Theology, or something that goes under that
name, is still kept alive by the faithful, but only by artificial respira-
tion. Its functions, the services it rendered in the time of St. Thomas,
have been taken over, not as is often supposed by philosophy, but
by history—the study of man and his world in the time sequence.
Theology in the thirteenth century presented the story of man and
the world according to the divine plan of salvation. It provided the
men of that age with an authentic philosophy of history, and they

could afford to ignore the factual experience of mankind since they were so well assured of its ultimate cause and significance. But in the succeeding centuries men turned more and more to an investigation of the recorded story of mankind, bringing to that enterprise a remarkable attention to detail, an ever greater preoccupation with the factual event. In the light of the mass of irreducible brute facts thus accumulated, the theological vision of man and his world faded into a pale replica of the original picture. In the eighteenth century the clear-cut theological philosophy of history had degenerated into an amiable and gentlemanly "philosophy teaching by example." In the early nineteenth century, history could still be regarded as the Transcendent Idea realizing itself in the actual. In our time, history is nothing but history, the notation of what has occurred, just as it happened. The object of history, according to Santayana, is quite simply "to fix the order of events throughout past times in all places." No respectable historian any longer harbors ulterior motives; and one who should surreptitiously introduce the gloss of a transcendent interpretation into the human story would deserve to be called a philosopher and straightway lose his reputation as a scholar.

I am, of course, using the word "history" in the broad sense. It is to be understood as a method of approach rather than as a special field of study. Literature and language, government and law, economics, science and mathematics, love and sport—what is there that has not in our time been studied historically? Much of what is called science is properly history, the history of biological or physical phenomena. The geologist gives us the history of the earth; the botanist relates the life history of plants. Professor Whitehead has recently illuminated physics by tracing the history of physical concepts. To regard all things in their historical setting appears, indeed, to be an instructive procedure of the modern mind. We do it without thinking, because we can scarcely think at all without doing it. The modern climate of opinion is such that we cannot seemingly understand our world unless we regard it as a going concern. We cannot properly know things as they are unless we know "how they came to be what they are." Nor is it merely, or chiefly, the succession of external events that engages our attention. No doubt St. Thomas was aware that one thing follows another. What is peculiar to the modern mind is the disposition and the determination to regard ideas and concepts, the truth of things as well as the things themselves, as changing entities, the character and significance of which at any given time can be fully grasped only by regarding them as points in an endless process of differentiation, of unfolding, of waste and repair. Let St. Thomas ask *us* to define anything—for example, the natural law—let him ask us to tell him what it *is*. We cannot do it. But, given time enough, we can relate for him its history. We can tell him what varied forms the natural law has assumed up to now. Historical-mindedness is so much a preconception of modern thought that we can identify a particular thing only by pointing to the various things it successively was before it became that particular thing which it will presently cease to be.

Besides the historical approach to knowledge we have another to which we are even more committed—the scientific. As history has gradually replaced theology, so science has replaced philosophy. Philosophy, it is true, has managed, much better than theology, to keep up appearances in the modern world, and at the present moment signs are not wanting of refurbishings going on in its ancient and somewhat dilapidated dwelling. Yet, it is obvious that the undisputed sway which it formerly exercised has long been usurped by natural science. In the hands of St. Thomas, philosophy, with "deductive" logic as its instrument of precision, was a method of building a rational world, its aim being to reconcile experience with revealed truth. But the influences which disposed succeeding generations to examine the facts of human history, induced them also to examine the facts of natural phenomena. The rise of history and of science were but two results of a single impulse, two aspects of the trend of modern thought away from an overdone rationalization of the facts to a more careful and disinterested examination of the facts themselves.

Galileo, for example (not that he was the first by any means), did not ask what Aristotle had said about falling bodies, or whether it was reasonable to suppose that a ten-pound weight would fall to the ground more quickly than a one-pound weight. He applied to this problem the scientific method. He dropped two weights, differing as ten to one, from the leaning tower, and noted the fact that both weights reached the ground at the same time. In such a world as this, he said in effect, this is the way falling bodies behave.

If that is not possible in a rational world, then the world we live in is not a rational one. Facts are primary and what chiefly concern us; they are stubborn and irreducible and we cannot get around them. They may be in accord with reason, let us hope that they are; but whether they are so or not is only a question of fact to be determined like any other.

This subtle shift in the point of view was perhaps the most important event in the intellectual history of modern times, but its implications were not at once understood. Philosophy continued to reign, and when in the eighteenth century she added a new word to her title (calling herself natural philosophy), no one noted the fact as ominous. Galileo and his successors were philosophers too, preëminently so, since their marvelous discoveries, based upon observation and experiment, uncovered so many secret places in the world, and by promising to banish mystery from the universe seemed to leave it more obviously rational than they found it. The laws of nature and nature's God appeared henceforth to be one and the same thing, and since every part of God's handiwork could all in good time be reasonably demonstrated, the intelligent man could very well do with a minimum of faith—except, of course (the exception was tremendous but scarcely noticed at the time), faith in the uniform behavior of nature and in the capacity of reason to discover its *modus operandi.*

In the course of the nineteenth century this optimistic outlook became overcast. The marriage of fact and reason, of science and the universal laws of nature, proved to be somewhat irksome, and in the twentieth century it was, not without distress, altogether dissolved. Natural philosophy was transformed into natural science. Natural science became science, and scientists rejected, as a personal affront, the title of philosopher, which formerly they had been proud to bear. The vision of man and his world as a neat and efficient machine, designed by an intelligent Author of the Universe, gradually faded away. Professors of science ceased to speak with any assurance of the laws of nature, and were content to pursue, with unabated ardor, but without any teleological implications whatever, their proper business of observing and experimenting with the something which is the stuff of the universe, of measuring and mastering its stress and movement. "Science," said Lloyd Morgan, "deals exclusively with changes of configuration, and traces the accelerations which are observed to occur, leaving to metaphysics to deal with the underlying agency, if it exist." [4]

It is well known that the result of pursuing this restricted aim (the scientific method reduced to its lowest terms) has been astounding. It is needless to say that we live in a machine age, that the art of inventing is the greatest of our inventions, or that within a brief space of fifty years the outward conditions of life have been transformed. It is less well understood that this bewildering experience has given a new slant to our minds. Fresh discoveries and new inventions are no longer the result of fortunate accidents which we are expected to note with awe. They are all a part of the day's work, anticipated, deliberately intended, and brought to pass according to schedule. Novelty has ceased to excite wonder because it has ceased to be novelty; on the contrary, the strange, so habituated have we become to it, is of the very essence of the customary. There is nothing new in heaven or earth not dreamt of in our laboratories; and we should be amazed indeed if tomorrow and tomorrow and tomorrow failed to offer us something new to challenge our capacity for readjustment. Science has taught us the futility of troubling to understand the "underlying agency" of the things we use. We have found that we can drive an automobile without knowing how the carburetor works, and listen to a radio without mastering the secret of radiation. We really haven't time to stand amazed, either at the starry firmament above or the Freudian complexes within us. The multiplicity of things to manipulate and make use of so fully engages our attention that we have neither the leisure nor the inclination to seek a rational explanation of the force that makes them function so efficiently.

In dismissing the underlying agency with a casual shrug, we are in good company. The high priest of science, even more than the common man, is a past master of this art. It is one of the engaging ironies of modern thought that the scientific method, which it was once fondly hoped would banish mystery from the world, leaves it every day more inexplicable. Physics, which it was thought had dispensed with the need of metaphysics, has been transformed by its own proper researches into the most metaphysical of disciplines. The more attentively the physicist looks at the material stuff of the world the less there is to see. Under his expert treatment the sub-

[4] *Interpretation of Nature,* p. 58.

stantial world of Newtonian physics has been dissolved into a complex of radiant energies. No efficient engineer or Prime Mover could have designed the world, since it can no longer be fully understood in terms of mechanics. "What is the sense of talking about a mechanical explanation," asks Professor Whitehead, "when you do not know what you mean by mechanics?" [5] We are told that if we ascribe position to anything it ceases to have determinable velocity; if we ascertain its velocity it ceases to have determinable position. The universe is said to be composed of atoms, an atom is said to be composed of a nucleus around which electrons revolve in determinable orbits; but experiments seem to show that an electron may, for reasons best known to itself, be moving in two orbits at the same time. To this point Galileo's common-sense method of noting the behavior of things, of sticking close to the observable facts, has brought us: it has at last presented us with a fact that common sense repudiates.

What can we do? Reason and logic cry out in pain no doubt; but we have long since learned not to bother overmuch with reason and logic. Logic was formerly visualized as something outside us, something existing independently which, if we were willing, could take us by the hand and lead us into the paths of truth. We now suspect that it is something the mind has created to conceal its timidity and keep up its courage, a hocus-pocus designed to give formal validity to conclusions we are willing to accept if everybody else in our set will too. If all men are mortal (an assumption), and if Socrates was a man (in the sense assumed), no doubt Socrates must have been mortal; but we suspect that we somehow knew all this before it was submitted to the test of a syllogism. Logics have a way of multiplying in response to the changes in point of view. First there was one logic, then there were two, then there were several; so that now, according to one authority (if a contributor to the *Encyclopaedia Britannica* who ventures to employ humor can be an authority), the state of logic is "that of Israel under the Judges, every man doeth that which is right in his own eyes." With all due allowance made for mathematical logic (which has to do with concepts, not with facts), and for the logic of probability (which Mr. Keynes assures us has a probable validity), the secure foundations of deductive and inductive logic have been battered to

[5] *Science and the Modern World*, p. 24.

pieces by the ascertainable facts, so that we really have no choice; we must cling to the ascertainable facts though they slay us.

Physicists, therefore, stick to the ascertainable facts. If logic presumes to protest in the name of the law, they know how to square it, so that it complaisantly looks the other way while they go on with illicit enterprises—with the business, for example (it is Sir William Bragg who vouches for it), of teaching "the wave theory of light on Monday, Wednesday, and Friday, and the quantum theory on Tuesday, Thursday, and Saturday." It need not surprise us, then, to learn that physicists make nothing, when it suits their convenience, of regarding nucleus and electron, not as substances, but only as radiations—thus, casually dissolving the substantial world into a congeries of repellent and attractive velocities which we are invited to believe in because they can be mathematically identified and made use of. Perhaps, as Professor Jeans suggests, the world we live in was designed by a mathematician. Why not, indeed, if it can be most easily understood in terms of mathematical formulas? We know that two apples plus two apples make four apples. We have always taken it for granted that the apples exist, but we can very well understand that even if no apples are anywhere found it still remains true that two plus two make four. The mathematician gets on just as well without the apples, better indeed, since the apples have other attributes besides number. When sufficiently hard pressed, therefore, the physicist solves his difficulties by turning mathematician. As mathematician he can calculate the velocities that are observed to occur, meantime assuring us that the velocities could readily be attributed to substantial electrons, provided substantial electrons with such velocities should ever turn up. There is really no occasion for despair: our world can be computed even if it doesn't exist.

Perhaps I have said enough to suggest that the essential quality of the modern climate of opinion is factual rather than rational. The atmosphere which sustains our thought is so saturated with the actual that we can easily do with a minimum of the theoretical. We necessarily look at our world from the point of view of history and from the point of view of science. Viewed historically, it appears to be something in the making, something which can at best be only tentatively understood since it is not yet finished. Viewed scientifically, it appears as something to be accepted, something to be manipulated and mastered, something to adjust ourselves to with the least possible stress. So long as we can make efficient use of things, we feel no irresistible need to understand them. No doubt it is for this reason chiefly that the modern mind can be so wonderfully at ease in a mysterious universe.

13 / FREEDOM FROM THE AUTHORITY OF LEGAL TRADITION

Jerome N. Frank's book Law and the Modern Mind, *published in 1930, is one of the most important and influential statements of that position among lawyers known as* legal realism. *Frank, born in 1889, graduated from the University of Chicago in 1909 and practiced law in Chicago and New York during the 1920's and 1930's. He also lectured at the Yale Law School and served in various capacities in the government until 1941, when he was appointed Judge of the United States Circuit Court of Appeals of New York. ¶Legal realism was a position taken in the 1930's by a very vocal minority of legal scholars centered primarily in the law schools, particularly in the Yale Law School. These men saw the advance of the social sciences— economics, sociology, anthropology, social psychology, political science—in the twentieth century, and sought to do the same for the "science of law." This group held that written constitutions and statutes were instruments of social engineering; they denied the existence of fundamental law and insisted upon an operational*

SOURCE: Jerome Frank, *Law and the Modern Mind* (New York: Anchor Books, 1963), pp. 246-52. Copyright 1930, 1933, 1949 by Coward McCann, Inc.; copyright 1930 by Brentano's, Inc.; copyright renewed in 1958 by Florence K. Frank. Reprinted by arrangement with the estate of Barbara Frank Kristein.

approach to law. Law, according to them, was what officials did. They pointed out the fact that, for litigants in any case, the judge's decision constitutes the law.

Now these common agreements as to "coercive experiences," these symposia with respect to the nature of Can't Helps, keep changing, even where the subject-matter has reference to what we call the laws of nature. In other words, stubborn facts are, in a sense, not so stubborn as we are wont to suppose. In the natural sciences the rate of change in the accepted symposia is rapid because there the habit of constant questioning, of unremitting doubt, has come to be accepted, at least by the scientists, as a virtue. Even in those sciences, it took thousands of years to justify doubt. And outside of the sciences, most of our facts have remained unchanged for at least several hundred generations. A large part of our accepted or unquestioned "truths" are the "unverified world-pictures of vanished barbaric (prehistoric) peoples." The toughness of these facts is due—to what? To the vast power of the authority behind them. They have become sacred; they are protected from close scrutiny by terrifying taboos.

Primitive man could not endure the terrors that surrounded him. He made masks to conceal the menace they involved, so that now, says Shaw, "every mask requires a hero to tear it off." [1] In each man's infancy, generation after generation, his father has taught him the eternal verity of these masking "truths." Wherefore he is coerced by them and treats them as if they were nature's irreducibles. And if the tendency to tear off the masks, to question man-made Can't Helps, has progressed far less rapidly in the law than in the natural sciences—if, that is, our "law facts" need to be brought in line with our "science facts"—this is no doubt because in the law father-authority has found a firmer lodgment.

This point is so important that we venture to state it once more in slightly variant terms. As we have often remarked . . . , our legal abstractions can only be approximations. They are, by definition, drawn off—abstracted—from the facts. Hence, the results

[1] "The Quintessence of Ibsenism," 20: "We have plenty of these masks around us still; some of them more fantastic than any of the Sandwich Islanders' masks in the British Museum."

can never be precise, perfect. They must be inexact. If the "environment" were stable, the degree of inexactness could become more negligible and remain relatively fixed.[2] But the economic, political and social problems are ever-shifting. So that, in the very nature of the situation, the approximations must be revised frequently and can never be accepted as final in terms of satisfactory consequences. We must be content with modest probabilities, as Dewey puts it, and not foolishly pretend that our legal abstractions are mathematically accurate, for that pretense obstructs the will to modify and adjust these abstractions in the light of careful observation of their working results.

These abstractions, that is to say, are tools whose whole value is instrumental. They have been contrived to meet particular problems. As new problems arise, the old tools must be adapted to cope with them. But when the old tools have been authoritatively pronounced to be once-and-for-all perfect, when, that is, they have the father-sanction, then to question their everlasting sufficiency is difficult. Then the tools seem not human contrivances but a very part of the nature of things. The questioning, when it begins, has to be oblique, the adaptions surreptitious. Even the questioner, the adapter, must not let himself know that he is daring to depart from the accepted ways. Science made large strides when man began to treat the traditional formulations as no longer completely correct and definite knowledge of objective nature but as hypotheses or fictions; in other words, when men were ready to treat as tentative the guesses about the external world which had been handed down to them. Then only could they fearlessly observe the events, dispassionately consider new guesses about the character of these events.

All the guesses are human and, therefore, subject to question. But the old guesses come to us as the father's truths and are, therefore, sacrosanct. Humanity increases its chances of survival and of progress to the extent that it becomes able to question—neither blindly to accept nor violently to defy—the father's guesses, and to discontinue calling them self-evident truths. In the sciences this attitude has won out. Although the law is a more patently human construction than, say, physics, yet, in the calm reconsideration of

[2] No complete rigidity would be attained, even so, unless and until the personalities of all judges became approximately uniform.

the value of inherited truths, law is decades behind physics. Why? Because in law, the father is more deeply entrenched. The law is a near substitute for that father, a belief in whose infallibility is essential to the very life of the child. And in the life of the adult that authority now no longer usefully, but still potently, often holds sway.

The fear of change is an ancient one. We may, with Elsie Clews Parsons, define civilization as man's steps in his escape from that fear. Whitehead puts the same thought somewhat differently: Development in life means wandering. Modern science has imposed on humanity the necessity for increased wandering, for migrations into uncharted seas. The future will disclose dangers. "It is the business of the future to be dangerous; and it is among the merits of science that it equips the future for its duties." We must not confuse civilization and security, for security and stability will, with advancing civilization, grow less. Too much insecurity is perhaps inconsistent with civilization. "But, on the whole, the great ages have been unstable ages."

Whence it follows that, if we are to grow more civilized, we must arrive at a more adult attitude towards chance and change. And here a nice distinction must be made between the adult position with respect to danger and a less developed sentiment which falsely resembles it.

Early in this essay we spoke of the bewilderment of the infant, of his seeking for sureness and security in the confused environment into which he has suddenly been ejected; of his finding, in a reliance upon his idealized father, some measure of relief from his confusion. And we traced the effects of the persistence in adult life of this reliance upon the father. But the child is motivated not only by the desire to escape the terrors of the unknown; he has also within him a store of vital energy, he is a growing dynamic organism. His dynamic capacities constantly assert themselves; the child is never completely a mere creature of parental authority. In a certain sense, danger and risk, as well as safety and security, make their appeal to him. As sometimes he runs away from chance and change, so at other times he seeks them.

Now the curious fact is that such childish courting of danger may be, in part, a product of father-authority. All children have a dual attitude towards the father. The child needs a belief in an all-powerful, all-wise parent. Yet that parent ever and again takes on the aspect of a harsh tyrant who cruelly and unfairly interferes with the child's aims and purposes. Even the most loving and obedient child feels occasional animosity towards the father and, at times, revolts against the father. His conduct, in such circumstances, may be in the direction of healthy growth, but, in so far as it is merely expressive of revolt, it is purely negative in meaning. The child, that is, may not be forging ahead, but only running away from a new terror—the terror of too strict fatherly authority.[3]

Recent writings in criminology have a decided bearing here. Many criminals, we learn, are driven to lawlessness by an inner, subconscious revolt against the authority of the father. In opposing the law they are reacting to it as a father-substitute. They, too, so to speak, demand (but "contrary-wise") an authoritarian law in order that they may rebel against it. Fatherly authority in their childhood was too oppressive and as a consequence the anti-authority bias developed as a determining conduct-factor throughout life.[4] The violent rebel against authority is no more "free" than the slave of authority; he is in bondage to a compulsion to revolt; his is a constrained attitude, which Cooley[5] has happily called the "subservience of contradiction." [6]

And so we must distinguish between that growth towards maturity which produces an acceptance of danger and that childish reaction against fatherly authority which takes on the appearance of adult

[3] M. D. Eder quotes a Japanese proverb which enumerates the four greatest terrors which Japan is called upon to endure: "Earthquakes, thunder, fire and too strict fatherly authority." The Freudians, in explaining the "ambivalent" attitude towards the father, properly consider other important factors which are not given attention here.
[4] One is reminded of those wretches in the Divine Comedy who "all the while felt themselves drawn onwards by a *fear which became a desire* towards the cruel riverside which awaits everyone destitute of the fear of God."
[5] "Life and the Student," 124.
[6] Compare Gilbert's observation:
> "I often think it's comical
> How nature always does contrive
> That every boy and every gal
> That's born into the world alive
> Is either a little Liberal
> Or else a little Conservative."

courage. The constrained rebellion against paternalism is not a symptom of development but of prolonged infantilism. It is another form of slavish obedience. The person engaged in such rebellion is not free of paternal authority, but is still subjectively dependent upon it.[7]

True growth involves healthy encouragement of the inherent spontaneity of the child, an encouragement of wakeful vitality and the discouragement of half-blind adherence to, or half-blind breaking away from, the traditional.

And so in law. If the search for the father-judge is ended,[8] if the authority-ridden mode of regarding law is eliminated, if men see law as a human adjustment and not as a gift or mandate from some external source, no violent transformation need or will occur. The relief from fear of chance need not result in the adoption of a policy of incessant, hectic change, but should lead to a policy of healthy and vital growth.

Today, excessive regard for certified stability yields to an excessive desire for modification, so that there is a constant unconscious struggle between these two impulses, a struggle unnecessarily violent. There is vacillation in the mind even of the average man between worship and denunciation of legal certainty. The demand for too much change is as little based on practicality as the demand for too much rigidity. Holmes has warned us that continuity with the past is not a duty. It is no less true that there is no obligation to effect discontinuity with the past. A recognition of those two truths, resulting from a thoroughly adult attitude towards fatherly authority, will produce a balanced, not an anarchic, attitude towards law.[9] When men are free of childish compulsions away from

[7] There is a measure of deep insight in the facetious remarks of Mr. Justice Darling: "I cannot avoid noticing an error into which they fall who complain of the uncertainty of law as though it were a weakness. Rather should it be considered the chiefest of all sanctions. . . . Many would dare to do wrong, did they know for certain what would follow."

[8] If the child indeed becomes father of the man, i.e., each individual becomes his own father and thus eliminates the need for fatherly authority.

[9] From the genetic point of view, development towards maturity might be roughly schematized as follows:

(1) At first the child's thinking is egocentric, "autistic," unsocialized. He accepts his own thoughts as self-evident; he is totally unaware of any subjectivity in his thinking. (2) Later, doubts arise as to the self-evident character

or towards the traditional, it will be possible for them to have an open mind on the question of the advisability of radical alterations of law.

In other words, such a revised attitude will not entail constant inquiry into the sufficiency of all legal formulations. *It is unnecessary and undesirable to attack on all fronts at once.* Certain formulations must have been and will be at any given moment treated as, for the time being, fixed and settled while others are being investigated. But those "rules" that are thus, for the time being, taken for granted, will be only temporarily dealt with as permanent. They will be considered as *temporary absolutes.* Some of them will be accepted because repeated checkings show them still to be working well;[10] others because the attention, at the moment, will be too occupied.[11]

Modern civilization demands a mind free of father-governance. To remain father-governed in adult years is peculiarly *the* modern sin. *The modern mind is a mind free of childish emotional drags, a mature mind.* And law, if it is to meet the needs of modern civilization, must adapt itself to the modern mind. It must cease to embody a philosophy opposed to change. It must become avowedly pragmatic. To this end there must be developed a recognition and

---

of his own thoughts. Their subjective character becomes somewhat apparent. He now substitutes the father's dogmas for his own. Father's thoughts are objectively real. (3) Still later, other authorities are substituted for the father. But, in this substitutive manner, fatherly authority still continues. Truths which emanate from authority are objectively real. (4) Then all authority may come into question, all human thought being conceived as subjective and therefore invalid and unreal. (5) The stage of complete maturity is reached when the relativity of all truths is accepted but seem to be compatible with the provisional validity and utility of such truths.

Once more, note that we are using a *"partial* explanation."

[10] Compare Dewey, "Human Nature and Conduct," 239.

[11] Whitehead has expressed this idea in generalized terms (loc. cit. 289): "There are two principles inherent in the very nature of things, recurring in some particular embodiments, whatever field we explore—the spirit of change, and the spirit of conservation. There can be nothing real without both. Mere change without conservation is a passage from nothing to nothing. Its final integration yields mere transient nonentity. Mere conservation without change cannot conserve. For after all, there is a flux of circumstance, and the freshness of being evaporates under mere repetition."

elimination of the carry-over of the childish dread of, and respect for, paternal omnipotence; that dread and respect are powerful strongholds of resistance to change. Until we become thoroughly cognizant of, and cease to be controlled by, the image of the father hidden away in the authority of the law, we shall not reach that first step in the civilized administration of justice, the recognition that man is not made for the law, but that the law is made by and for men.

14 / FREEDOM FROM OBJECTIVE AUTHORITY

Charles A. Beard, historian, political scientist, and publicist, as versatile as he was prolific, lived his life amid controversy, much of which he stimulated himself. He was born in 1874 in the Midwest and studied in England, where he became involved with the Fabian socialists. His first book, The Industrial Revolution, *appeared in England in 1901. His interest shifted to American history after taking his Ph.D. at Columbia, where he became a member of the history faculty. He pioneered in the analysis of the economic roots of political behavior in his book,* An Economic Interpretation of the Constitution of the United States *(1913). In 1918 he resigned his post at Columbia in protest over the invasion of academic freedom.   ¶In the late twenties Beard became interested in the philosophic foundations of historical knowledge. He is most noted among historians for his formulation of a relativistic position that was most fully stated in his* American Historical Review *essay of 1935, "That Noble Dream." However, he was concerned not merely with history but with all of the social sciences and attacked those social scientists who maintained that their own*

SOURCE: Charles A. Beard, *The Nature of the Social Sciences in Relation to Objectives of Instruction,* pp. 38-49. Copyright 1934 Charles Scribner's Sons and reprinted with their permission; renewal copyright © 1962 William A. Beard.

values and predilections had no bearing upon the gathering, selection, and interpretation of their data. Beard, in writing The Nature of the Social Sciences in Relation to Objectives of Instruction *(1934), was acting as a member of the Commission on Social Studies of the American Historical Association, which represented a massive effort on the part of social scientists to reconstitute the social studies in the schools.*

In our survey of social thought we also encounter another type—humanistic thought concerned with the good and the beautiful. The student of science may theoretically close his mind to this type of thought and these considerations, but the fact of their existence remains. In truth, it may be said that the historic books which have furnished most of the ideas and substance on which empirical refinements have been constructed have not been *neutral* presentations of knowledge and thought, leaning neither to the right nor to the left. Plato, Aristotle, Machiavelli, Locke, Rousseau, Adam Smith, Hamilton, Madison, Ricardo, J. S. Mill, Spencer, Bagehot, Marx, and Comte were not mere empiricists, indifferent to all values and purposes. Intrinsically, the works of these authors, however factual in character, are pleas for certain views of society and certain choices as to purposes and policies and actions. They are not collections of authentic data poised in perfect balance. They are forward-thrusting assertions of values or preferences to be attained by choice and action.

Some of these great treatises are more ethical in motive than others; Plato's *Republic* is more idealistic than Aristotle's *Politics;* but in none of them, not even in the cold realism of Machiavelli, are good or better ends repudiated and dropped out of sight. Moreover, in works purely empirical in pretension, conceptions of value appear, in the choice of the subject to be treated, the selection of materials, the organization of materials, and the conclusions, either openly or implicitly.

Many contemporary scholars in the social sciences will, no doubt, vigorously combat the idea that they have anything to do with ethics and esthetics, with purposes and utilities. They are engaged, they may say, in the disinterested pursuit of truth and it is not their business to write prescriptions for mankind vexed by social ills. Having witnessed the follies of many thinkers who proclaim codes of morals without fear and without research, having seen many an ideal shattered on the cruel rocks of reality, they shrink from playing the role of prophet and leader. That role is beset with intellectual difficulties and is perilous in many ways besides. So these scholars choose another course. They devote themselves in the scientific spirit to particular enterprises, such as the study of Cæsar's campaigns in Gaul or the English grain trade in the sixteenth century, without troubling themselves about the value of their work to anybody else. Having practiced the art in a narrow area, they assume that it is generally applicable and that they are following a program consistent in itself.

This has been called the spirit of "idle curiosity." In the physical sciences it has undoubtedly accomplished extraordinary results and in the particulars of the social sciences it has brought forth knowledge of the utmost value to mankind, by illuminating particular areas of custom and conduct. But in the organization of the social sciences the spirit of idle curiosity, pure and undefiled by thought of utility, cannot operate. Every individual who indulges in it is in fact a personality of many sides and belongs to a particular society and age. He finds leisure for pursuing the quest either because society has provided him with a living or because he is able to make a living in a way that affords a certain amount of leisure. He is not a disembodied spirit of idle curiosity operating in a vacuum. Usually, if not always, he chooses a special subject of inquiry with reference to throwing light on some problem or set of problems; indeed it is almost impossible to select any topic involving human beings which presents to the mind no implications wider than the specific subject matter. And the investigator brings to the consideration of any subject his own mentality which is inevitably that of an age, a nation, a class, or some social grouping. Hence an escape from some conception of good or better is almost if not entirely out of the question for the investigator, however narrow the range of the topic he has chosen for treatment.

The larger the theme the more inevitable the ethical implications, even though the most rigorous empiricism is applied to the inquiry. In any system of history, political science, economics, or sociology the frame-work of thought and method which the author brings to bear on the totality, on the selecting and organizing of facts, will make its impress. Its existence may be denied, it may be nebulous, but it is there, nevertheless. If the author succeeds in giving to his work the appearance of cold and neutral rationality, the appearance will be penetrated by those aware of the subjective factors entering into all intellectual constructions and acquainted with the types of thought and emphasis appropriate to different classes and ages. It will be found on inquiry that the author does in fact have more or less decided views about the ideal implications of his work, although he may not express them vividly in his written text. So we cannot avoid the conclusion that all treatises in the field of the social sciences which have any degree of generality carry within themselves ethical conceptions, expressly or tacitly, and that pretensions to complete neutrality and indifference do not correspond exactly to the realities of the case.

If, in spite of such evident facts, it is urged that the social sciences as sciences should not be concerned at all with the ideal, with good or better, writers in this field must admit that the human beings in society do have desires, interests, hopes, admirations, and that they make choices. In other words ethics, that is, the choice of objects of desire, is based on values; this end is good or is better than another. The social scientist may declare, if he wishes, that he will ignore this continuous process of valuing or choosing that goes on in society, which makes for the change of culture by discarding the old and adding the new, but by his declaration he merely shuts his eyes to a large part of the "data" of his field, essential and determining data. Any science thus limited is, as Ruskin says, akin to a science of gymnastics which assumes that men have no skeletons. "It might be shown, on that supposition, that it would be advantageous to roll the students up into pellets, flatten them into cakes, or stretch them into cables; and then when these results were effected, the reinsertion of the skeleton would be attended with various inconveniences to their constitution. The reasoning might be admirable, the conclusions true, and the science deficient only in applicability." So it is with any social science which rules out of account all operations of choice, value, or preference and assumes that human beings are atoms in a physical complex. It may be admirably logical in its construction and conclusions; it is deficient in applicability.

Should social scientists still insist on having nothing to do with value judgments—a thing theoretically possible but practically impossible—they must be reminded of two unequivocal facts in the situation. The first is that the greatest among their colleagues from Plato to John A. Hobson, from Aristotle to John Maynard Keynes, have faced the realities of their subject with wide comprehension and have not shrunk from making value judgments themselves. The second is that, if those who are most informed about the data of the social sciences will make no such judgments deliberately, thinkers and doers in actual life, confronting competing values, will and must make decisions. Human desires, interests, hopes, admirations, dislikes, and resentments will not disappear because social scientists refuse to take them into consideration and ostentatiously decline to express any opinions respecting them. Humanity will continue to make history, although the skeptical historian can find no reason why it should be done. Even Aristotle, who reacted against the idealism of Plato and had a deep respect for facts, recognized this truth and came to the conclusion that, despite the appearances of confusion and evil, statesmen were achieving a certain approximation to an ideal of some kind.

Indeed this is among the fundamental data of the social sciences: the conduct of human beings in society approximates an ideal of some kind. The humblest housewife does try to make her home attain a certain good or at least she does not seek to make it as bad as possible. The humblest farmer, amid the most distressing circumstances, does attempt to make his fields and garden approximate some ideal of excellence. Were this striving for an ideal, for good or better, to disappear from the human spirit, the race would sink into barbarism and ultimately disappear. Even the barbarian is not content with being as dirty, nasty, and degraded as possible within the limits of a miserable existence. At all events, the various steps in the advancement of mankind, as individuals, and as societies, are marked by aspirations for a certain good or a certain better. Belittling or ignoring these aspirations may put a damper on aspirations, but it cannot eradicate them, at least while society continues to exist and function.

Any particular social scientist, sitting comfortably in his study, housed, clothed, and fed by society, may, of course, formally abstain from taking any part in the conflicts of society over values and aspirations although actually by his conduct, if not by his words, he lends sanction to this or that ethical conception. But citizens, school boards, and teachers in the real world of stress and contest do daily make choices, arrive at decisions, and act on ethical assumptions: this is good or better than the other thing or line of action. It cannot be denied that making such value judgments and decisions in many departments of life—family, economic, and political—is hazardous business. The good or better set up by one person may be denied or trampled upon by others; or the course chosen may produce unexpected or undesired results. Nevertheless in such hazards is life entangled; and nothing is gained by refusing to face the facts. Only the formalism of scholasticism can refuse to face them. In life they cannot be avoided, and if the social sciences have any relation to life they must confront these hazards also.

The social sciences, then, are ethical sciences. Although one school may claim formally that they are as neutral as the physical sciences, another school will openly and frankly recognize the ethical nature and implications of their intellectual operations. As ethical sciences they are concerned with good or better conduct and good or better material and social arrangements. Near the center of ethics are material arrangements necessary to the continuance of life—the practical arts related to the production of food, clothing, shelter, and the amenities of civilization. Without these things life cannot go on at all; but they are not ends; they are means to life. The practical arts include both material things—raw materials, tools, and machines—and talents or capacities for making effective use of them. Even the practical arts rest upon moral capacities, such as loyalty, industry, persistence, reliability, and dependability. Thus certain propensities and forms of conduct are necessary to the functioning of the practical arts upon which all life depends for its existence. Machines do not dictate their uses to mankind; their uses depend upon the cultural heritage and aspirations of the users. If every manager, engineer, artisan, and worker sought to do the worst he could instead of some good or better, organized industry would obviously be impossible. That much seems beyond argument.

Nor can social life not directly related to the practical arts continue unless whole masses of people have some common conceptions of good and realize them more or less perfectly in practice. A social scientist may regard the action of a bad boy in yelling "fire" at a theater as a mere "phenomenon" for study; but the rest of the audience in the theater will take a different view of the matter; so, too, with the social scientist if he is in the audience and near the bad boy. Now it cannot be denied that these conceptions of social good vary widely, but they must overlap or agree near some central points; otherwise social life would disintegrate. The task of finding this center, of defining the area of liberty on the periphery, is not easy, but it is categorical for all those concerned with the existence and progressive development of society, for those who keep society going. This task may and should be undertaken in the spirit of pure science, but the objective is ethical in upshot, if not in the intention of the investigator.

Intrinsically involved in ethics is esthetics, the reality and science of beauty. Despite all theorizing about art for art's sake, esthetics is not a matter of mere personal "expression" or meretricious adornment, as sometimes supposed. It is connected with the practical arts of life—the form, shape, and colors of objects produced by industry, the architecture of buildings, the layout of roads and streets, and the serving of food at the table. Such things are classed as "good" or "bad," according to tastes and predilections. Standards differ widely of course, but all people high and low have some standards; none seeks to make things as ugly as he possibly can in terms of his own standards. Esthetics is also connected with conduct, for conduct may be graceful or awkward, that is, beautiful or ugly. Finally civilizations themselves may be measured with reference to prevailing standards of beauty and to the wide prevalence of beauty in material layout, objects of use and adornment, and social conduct. The neutral social scientist may regard the slums, filth, and distress of great industrial cities as inevitable, or merely as interesting social phenomena, but he will scarcely call them beautiful. Civilizations cannot be graded solely with respect to the *number* of things found in them; esthetic standards are inevitably involved. Thus even wealth, with which economics deals, does not consist in a given amount of commodities which can be exchanged, but, as Ruskin says, in "the possession of the valuable by the valiant," by people capable of making effective, good, and beautiful use of it. What alternative can be offered by social science, either neutral or ethical?

If the foregoing statements are valid in essence, it is evident that the formulation of purposes and means of instruction in the social sciences must proceed on ethical and esthetic assumptions with all due respect for the necessities of every situation disclosed by empirical inquiry. And when these ethical and esthetic assumptions are visualized they will take the form of an ideal of material things, social arrangements, and personal conduct, more or less positively and accurately conceived. The bolder the thinker and the profounder his observations, the clearer and more realistic will be his frame of reference, or ideal to be realized, to which objectives and means of instruction will be related. To attempt the impossible would be utopian, though perhaps not without its uses; to attempt less than the best that is possible would be to betray knowledge.

SUMMARY

The findings of this inquiry into the general nature of the social sciences may be summarized in the following formulas:

1. The social sciences embrace large bodies of organized and authentic knowledge respecting human affairs—knowledge, which is absolutely indispensable to the conduct of individual life, the management of economies, the government of nations, and the adjustment of international relations. Deprived of these bodies of knowledge, modern civilization would sink down into primitive barbarism. The more complex contemporary life becomes the more indispensable are the social sciences to the continuance and advancement of civilization.

2. The empirical or scientific method employed in the social sciences is a precious and necessary instrument for the accumulation and authentication of knowledge and for drawing conclusions, especially in areas of social data peculiarly susceptible to mathematical treatment. Competent conduct and administration in private affairs, industry, agriculture, and government—local, state, and national—are based upon findings of fact and upon rules or axioms drawn from the study and observation of social actualities and records. This remains true, although there has been created no real

science of society or of any division of society, political or economic.

3. Being neutral in essence and limited in its application to social affairs, empiricism can deliver no mandates to society or education, however indispensable it may be as an instrument of human purpose and exploration. What *should* happen is a matter of indifference to it. If it were thought "desirable" by empiricists to teach only facts empirically established and the empirical method itself, the idea could not be realized in practice because valuations would inevitably enter into the selection and organization of the facts to be taught. Indeed the very idea is a contradiction in terms, for the scientist as such has no preferences or conceptions of desirability.

4. When the whole range of the social sciences or, more properly speaking, social knowledge and thought, is taken into consideration, it is found to embrace more than fragments empirically established. The most influential works, such as Adam Smith's *Wealth of Nations* or the *Federalist* by Hamilton, Madison, and Jay, are not empirical or neutral sciences, but assert human values deemed desirable and are arguments for the establishment of institutions and practices calculated to realize the values chosen and asserted. Moreover, the more general and formal treatises in history, political science, economics, and sociology, which profess neutrality as to all values, reveal in the selection and organization of materials conceptions of value, either hidden or openly expressed. Although the authors may have rigorously employed the empirical method, these treatises manifest preferences in selection, arrangement, and emphasis, which are at bottom judgments of value. Hence the social sciences broadly conceived are ethical sciences, not empirical, natural, or neutral sciences. Contemporary thought about the social sciences admits of no other conclusion respecting their essential nature.

5. If the above findings are true and they seem to be, then we may come to a conclusion respecting the "offerings" of the social sciences to those who are determining the purposes and means of instruction in the social studies. In two fundamental respects, social sciences and natural sciences are akin. (1) Neither group has been able to make an all-embracing and final philosophy of the subject matters under its consideration and (2) neither group as a body of empirical thought can declare the *uses* to which its findings of fact and law *should* be put by mankind. In one fundamental respect the social sciences are different: they include within their scope

actualities, knowledge, and thought bearing directly on ethical and esthetic purposes in human affairs. As empirical sciences, they can present the systems of ethics and esthetics from which, within limits, individuals, communities, groups, and nations may make choices of good, better, and best, although they cannot manufacture a final system of ethics and esthetics which must, by its own nature, be imposed upon mankind, as the law of gravitation is imposed on the architect. Using the methods of empirical and scholarly research, they can disclose, in broad outlines, the circumstances which make possible what happens and which partly determine and partly condition human action and the results that flow from it. Thus, while the social sciences present something less than a picture of the ultimate design of the universe, they offer to mankind knowledge, thought, and a method absolutely indispensable to the construction, maintenance, and advancement of civilization, and to all the detailed operations incidental to that great process.

PART IV

The Quest for Moral Freedom

(1941-1965)

THE TRAUMA of the Second World War and the subsequent Cold War touched off a reaction to the relativism of the 1930's and a search for a moral basis for freedom and the control of limitless power. Although the reasons for such a reaction are numerous, they are not difficult to find. The fascist states in the 1930's violated basic American values of individual freedom and human dignity, not to mention due process of law. Americans looked with growing horror upon totalitarianism, as events crowded one upon another: the Italian invasion of Ethiopia; the Nazis' wholesale extermination of Jews; violations of treaties; and the communist purge trials of 1938 which made a mockery of Western concepts of justice. The invasion of Poland, the attack on Pearl Harbor, and finally our own violation of the rights of citizens with the internment of Japanese-Americans—all demonstrated the effects of unrestrained power.

A new and more awesome element entered the picture with the explosions over Hiroshima and Nagasaki, signaling the harnessing of elemental force—atomic energy. The advent of the atomic bomb was the climax of man's long struggle to control his natural environment. He now had the power to destroy the world. This was an absolute, a certainty that many people came to recognize. The question was whether man could control himself. The question increased in urgency as Americans grudgingly acknowledged that the eternal struggle for power had not ended with the defeat of Germany and Japan. The existence of a long Cold War brought realization of the desperate necessity to control power, to set bounds for the struggle for primacy in the world, and a new awareness of the meager means for such controls.

Evidence of the coming reaction began with the invasion of Poland, as legal realists Karl Lewellyn and Jerome Frank beat a rapid retreat from their earlier positions. They now affirmed the existence of a universal law and argued that "the goal of the law is justice, and judges, like other officials, are not free to be arbitrary. . . ." In 1945, Supreme Court Justice Robert Jackson launched a vigorous attack on the legal realists and a year later was chosen to represent the United States as prosecutor at the war crimes trials held in Nuremberg, Germany, an event that underscored a renewed faith in the existence of a universal moral law to which all men can be held accountable. Physicists carried on a most unpositivistic debate over their moral responsibilities as men for what they did as scientists. Functionalist anthropologists, or cultural relativists, like Bronislaw Malinowski and Clyde Kluckhohn, turned their attention to a search for cultural similarities as evidence of universal values. In the Brown case of 1954 (Selection 16), the Supreme Court dramatically launched a concerted drive to build new supports for civil rights and broaden the area of individual freedom. There was also a concurrent resurgence of political conservatism and religious ferment. Carl Becker turned back to history in search of universal values (Selection 15). Existential philosophy with its emphasis on the uniqueness of the individual had an explosive vogue among American college students and intellectuals. Reinhold Niebuhr, once a voice crying in the wilderness, now became the popular spokesman for Protestant neo-orthodoxy (Selection 17). Even such an unrepentant behaviorist as B. F. Skinner pointed out the need for some means to check the irresponsible use of new psychological techniques for manipulating men (Selection 18). The quest of the postwar years, then, has been for a moral basis for freedom in an apparently immoral world.

15 / THE SEARCH FOR VALUES IN HISTORY

*In the late twenties and early thirties, Becker emphasized
the fallibility of the historian and the absurdity of his
pretensions to objectivity and certainty. Toward the
end of the 1930's, he began to see that the logical outcome
of a crude relativist position was an equally dangerous
fallacy: the assumption that because truth is in some
sense relative, it cannot be distinguished from error. By
1940, as Hitler's divisions swept victoriously over Europe,
Becker came to believe that it mattered very much that
all men should care what happened, and why. It
seemed to him that what men must care about to save
themselves in 1940 was the faith Becker himself had
helped to undermine—the faith in reason, in objective
fact, in the honest pursuit of truth. Reason, he argued,
had a function, and that was to discriminate the
relatively true from the relatively false, based on a
yardstick of universal values. He sought these values
in an analysis of history.*

IV

The trend of thought variously known as anti-intellectualism, relativism, activism, assumes its crudest and least defensible form in
the dictum of Thrasymachus that "might makes right, justice is
the interest of the stronger." For more than half a century this
doctrine, in more or less diluted form, has slowly, insidiously, not
altogether unashamed, warped itself into the fabric of democratic
thought and practice; and now, under pressure of economic col-
lapse and social frustration, it has been exalted to the level of a
complete philosophy of life in certain countries which have frankly
abandoned democratic institutions. In their theoretical exposition

SOURCE: Carl L. Becker, "Some Generalities That Still Glitter," Chapter V in
New Liberties for Old (New Haven: Yale University Press, 1941), pp. 144-51.

of ultimate aims, both communism and fascism pay tribute to certain ideal values—the welfare and happiness of the community, the progress of mankind—which are assumed to be in some mystical fashion identified with an abstract entity, called in the one case the dialectic of history, in the other the totalitarian state. Yet both assume that the abstract entity is realized in the activities of an inspired leader to whom the truth has been revealed and the direction of affairs committed; and as they exhibit themselves in action under the leader both represent a direct attack upon intelligence, an unqualified denial of any obligation to be guided by rational thinking or humane dealing. Both assume that the individual man has no importance except as an instrument to be used, with whatever degree of brutality may be necessary, for the common good as the leader understands it. Both subordinate reason to will, identify law and morality with naked force as an instrument of will, and accord value to the disinterested search for truth only in so far as the leader judges it to be momentarily useful for the attainment of immediate political ends. Herein the anti-intellectual, relativist trend of thought reaches a final, fantastic form: truth and morality turn out to be relative to the purposes of any egocentric somnambulist who can succeed, by a ruthless projection of his personality, in creating the power to impose his unrestrained will upon the world.

Hitler and Stalin represent an exorbitant price for a little wisdom. But they have at least done something to strengthen the cause of democracy. More than anything else in recent years, their incredible sophistries and ruthless brutalities have revealed to us the advantages of democratic institutions and the reality of the rational and humane values that are traditionally associated with them. The Declaration of Independence may now be referred to without apology, and even policemen on the beat are becoming dimly aware that there is such a thing as the Bill of Rights. What associations for the defense of civil liberties could not accomplish, Hitler and Stalin have in some measure accomplished; and they have accomplished it by frankly accepting, ruthlessly applying, and thereby reducing to an absurdity the principle that law and morality are nothing more than the right of the stronger.

The absurdity is that this principle, accepted with the moral obtuseness and applied with the cynical brutality of the Hitlers and the Stalins, eliminates from the world those rational and humane values which for more than two thousand years men have commonly accepted as the test of civilized living, however little their actual conduct may have conformed to them. The exertion of brute force is a fact which we cannot ignore; but to justify the brute fact by its existence and pressure is to end with no means of distinguishing fact from illusion, since illusion is a fact the existence of which is undeniable and the pressure of which may be immense. Might and right are discordant and incommensurable terms, and while it is necessary to submit to that which is stronger, there is nothing which men have more persistently or universally denied than that it is right to approve of it for that reason. To say that justice is the right of the stronger is to dispense with right and justice altogether. There is then nothing but the fact, or rather nothing but what is, which is neither good nor bad, fact nor illusion, but merely that which is "existential," as the philosophers say. There is then no place for law or morality. There is then no place for reason, even as an instrument functionally developed to serve the interest of a biological organism. For if reason is a functional instrument, then it must have a function, and what function can it have if it be not to discriminate the relatively true from the relatively false, the dependable fact from the deceptive illusion, in order that the organism may pursue the better rather than the less good interest? Granted that reason is an instrument developed to serve the interest of the organism, the chief service it can perform is to determine which of many interests it is best for the organism to pursue. The choice in any particular instance may be a good one, but whether it is so or not cannot be determined by the fact that the organism has chosen to respond to a purely egoistic impulse and has exhibited the power required to gratify it.

It does not matter that we cannot share the belief of an earlier generation in the easy triumph of the right-thinking man. We may still believe in his triumph. We may admit that mind is an integral part of the animal organism, and that the pronouncements of reason are subtly shaped by subconscious desire and emotion. We may admit it, and we should admit it gladly, since to know the limitations of reason is to increase its power in the long run. If we know (and we knew it long before Freud) that the wish is father to the thought, that the heart has reasons that reason knows not of, it was, after all, reason that revealed this secret to us, and the secret, once revealed, enables reason to avoid illusions that would otherwise vitiate its conclusions. The fallacy is to suppose that because truth is in some sense relative it cannot be distinguished from error, or that the margin of error cannot be progressively reduced. The fallacy is to suppose that reason cannot transcend its lowly animal origin, to suppose that because it is a function of the organism's total activity and can be and is employed in the service of purely egoistic and brutal impulses, it cannot serve purposes of a more humane and impersonal import. On the contrary, whatever success men have had since the Stone Age in lifting themselves above the level of brute existence has been the result of the slowly developing capacity of reason to distinguish fact from illusion and to prefer the values that exalt the humane and rational qualities of the human personality to the values that deny and degrade them.

To have faith in the dignity and worth of the individual man as an end in himself, to believe that it is better to be governed by persuasion than by coercion, to believe that fraternal good will is more worthy than a selfish and contentious spirit, to believe that in the long run all values are inseparable from the love of truth and the disinterested search for it, to believe that knowledge and the power it confers should be used to promote the welfare and happiness of all men rather than to serve the interests of those individuals and classes whom fortune and intelligence endow with temporary advantage—these are the values which are affirmed by the traditional democratic ideology. But they are older and more universal than democracy and do not depend upon it. They have a life of their own apart from any particular social system or type of civilization. They are the values which, since the time of Buddha and Confucius, Solomon and Zoroaster, Plato and Aristotle, Socrates and Jesus, men have commonly employed to measure the advance or the decline of civilization, the values they have celebrated in the saints and sages whom they have agreed to canonize. They are the values that readily lend themselves to rational justification, yet need no justification. No one ever yet found it necessary to justify a humane and friendly act by saying that it was really a form of brutality and oppression; but the resort to coercion in civil government, in war and revolution, in the exploitation of the poor or the liquidation of the rich, has always to be justified by saying that the apparent evil is an indirect means of achieving the greater or the ultimate good. Even the Hitlers and the Stalins, in order to win the support of their own people, find it necessary to do lip service to the humane values, thus paying the customary tribute of hypocrisy which virtue exacts from vice.

Whatever the limitations of reason may be, it is folly to renounce it, since it is the only guide we have—the only available means of enlarging the realm of scientific knowledge, the only means of discriminating the social value of the various uses to which such knowledge may be put. Whatever the limitations of reason may be, they are not so great that the civilized man cannot recognize the existence and the necessity of naked force and coercion in an imperfect social world, without attributing to them the creation of those humane and rational values which by their very nature affirm that naked force and coercion are at best necessary evils.

The case for democracy is that it accepts the rational and humane values as ends, and proposes as the means of realizing them the minimum of coercion and the maximum of voluntary assent. We may well abandon the cosmological temple in which the democratic ideology originally enshrined these values without renouncing the faith it was designed to celebrate. The essence of that faith is belief in the capacity of man, as a rational and humane creature, to achieve the good life by rational and humane means. The chief virtue of democracy, and the sole reason for cherishing it, is that with all its faults it still provides the most favorable conditions for achieving that end by those means.

16 / FUNDAMENTAL LAW REASSERTED

In this unanimous opinion of the Supreme Court, the case questioned the validity of state laws providing for racial segregation in the public schools. It climaxed a series of cases in which the Court dealt with segregation in law schools and graduate schools, striking down segregation on the basis of specific inequalities. It was not

SOURCE: Brown v. Board of Education, 341 U.S. 494 (1954).

until the Brown case that the Court dealt directly with the doctrine of "separate but equal" evolved from the Plessy v. Ferguson decision, and indirectly with the moral question of racial segregation. The Court, following the acceptance of the Brandeis Brief in Muller v. Oregon, based its decision on social data rather than legal logic. The Justices pointed to several psychological studies demonstrating that the inevitable consequence of segregation backed by law was a numbing sense of inferiority on the part of the colored child. Therefore, the Court argued, current psychological knowledge demonstrated that even though the physical facilities and other tangible factors might be equal, "separate educational facilities are inherently unequal." Although there are no overt references to ethics or to a moral code the technical phrasing of the opinion barely conceals the fact that the Justices looked upon the question as a moral issue. Here was an instance to be followed by a whole succession of civil rights cases where power was disciplined by moral ideals, supported by knowledge gained through behavioral sciences.

BROWN ET AL. *v.* BOARD OF EDUCATION
OF TOPEKA ET AL.

NO. 1. APPEAL FROM THE UNITED STATES DISTRICT COURT
FOR THE DISTRICT OF KANSAS.

Argued December 9, 1952.—Reargued December 8, 1953.—
Decided May 17, 1954.

. . . . .

MR. CHIEF JUSTICE WARREN delivered the opinion of the Court.

These cases come to us from the States of Kansas, South Carolina, Virginia, and Delaware. They are premised on different facts and different local conditions, but a common legal question justifies their consideration together in this consolidated opinion.[1]

[1] In the Kansas case, *Brown v. Board of Education,* the plaintiffs are Negro children of elementary school age residing in Topeka. They brought this action in the United States District Court for the District of Kansas to enjoin

enforcement of a Kansas statute which permits, but does not require, cities of more than 15,000 population to maintain separate school facilities for Negro and white students. Kan. Gen. Stat. § 72-1724 (1949). Pursuant to that authority, the Topeka Board of Education elected to establish segregated elementary schools. Other public schools in the community, however, are operated on a nonsegregated basis. The three-judge District Court, convened under 28 U.S.C. §§ 2281 and 2284, found that segregation in public education has a detrimental effect upon Negro children, but denied relief on the ground that the Negro and white schools were substantially equal with respect to buildings, transportation, curricula, and educational qualifications of teachers. 98 F. Supp. 797. The case is here on direct appeal under 28 U.S.C. § 1253.

In the South Carolina case, *Briggs* v. *Elliott,* the plaintiffs are Negro children of both elementary and high school age residing in Clarendon County. They brought this action in the United States District Court for the Eastern District of South Carolina to enjoin enforcement of provisions in the state constitution and statutory code which require the segregation of Negroes and whites in public schools. S.C. Const., Art. XI, § 7; S.C. Code § 5377 (1942). The three-judge District Court, convened under 28 U.S.C. §§ 2281 and 2284, denied the requested relief. The court found that the Negro schools were inferior to the white schools and ordered the defendants to begin immediately to equalize the facilities. But the court sustained the validity of the contested provisions and denied the plaintiffs admission to the white schools during the equalization program. 98 F. Supp. 529. This Court vacated the District Court's judgment and remanded the case for the purpose of obtaining the court's views on a report filed by the defendants concerning the progress made in the equalization program. 342 U.S. 350. On remand, the District Court found that substantial equality had been achieved except for buildings and that the defendants were proceeding to rectify this inequality as well. 103 F. Supp. 920. The case is again here on direct appeal under 28 U.S.C. § 1253.

In the Virginia case, *Davis* v. *County School Board,* the plaintiffs are Negro children of high school age residing in Prince Edward County. They brought this action in the United States District Court for the Eastern District of Virginia to enjoin enforcement of provisions in the state constitution and statutory code which require the segregation of Negroes and whites in public schools. Va. Const., § 140; Va. Code § 22-221 (1950). The three-judge District Court, convened under 28 U.S.C. §§ 2281 and 2284, denied the requested relief. The court found the Negro school inferior in physical plant, curricula, and transportation, and ordered the defendants forthwith to provide substantially equal curricula and transportation and to "proceed with all reasonable diligence and dispatch to remove" the inequality in physical plant. But, as in the South Carolina case, the court sustained the validity of the contested provisions and denied the plaintiffs admission to the white schools during the equalization program. 103 F. Supp. 337. The case is here on direct appeal under 28 U.S.C. § 1253.

In the Delaware case, *Gebhart* v. *Belton,* the plaintiffs are Negro children

In each of the cases, minors of the Negro race, through their legal representatives, seek the aid of the courts in obtaining admission to the public schools of their community on a nonsegregated basis. In each instance, they had been denied admission to schools attended by white children under laws requiring or permitting segregation according to race. This segregation was alleged to deprive the plaintiffs of the equal protection of the laws under the Fourteenth Amendment. In each of the cases other than the Delaware case, a three-judge federal district court denied relief to the plaintiffs on the so-called "separate but equal" doctrine announced by this Court in *Plessy* v. *Ferguson,* 163 U.S. 537. Under that doctrine, equality of treatment is accorded when the races are provided substantially equal facilities, even though these facilities be separate. In the Delaware case, the Supreme Court of Delaware adhered to that doctrine, but ordered that the plaintiffs be admitted to the white schools because of their superiority to the Negro schools.

The plaintiffs contend that segregated public schools are not "equal" and cannot be made "equal," and that hence they are deprived of the equal protection of the laws. Because of the obvious importance of the question presented, the Court took jurisdiction.[2]

---

of both elementary and high school age residing in New Castle County. They brought this action in the Delaware Court of Chancery to enjoin enforcement of provisions in the state constitution and statutory code which require the segregation of Negroes and whites in public schools. Del. Const., Art. X, § 2; Del. Rev. Code § 2631 (1935). The Chancellor gave judgment for the plaintiffs and ordered their immediate admission to schools previously attended only by white children, on the ground that the Negro schools were inferior with respect to teacher training, pupil-teacher ratio, extracurricular activities, physical plant, and time and distance involved in travel. 87 A. 2d 862. The Chancellor also found that segregation itself results in an inferior education for Negro children (see note 10, *infra*), but did not rest his decision on that ground. *Id.,* at 865. The Chancellor's decree was affirmed by the Supreme Court of Delaware, which intimated, however, that the defendants might be able to obtain a modification of the decree after equalization of the Negro and white schools had been accomplished. 91 A. 2d 137, 152. The defendants, contending only that the Delaware courts had erred in ordering the immediate admission of the Negro plaintiffs to the white schools, applied to this Court for certiorari. The writ was granted, 344 U.S. 891. The plaintiffs, who were successful below, did not submit a cross-petition.
[2] 344 U.S. 1, 141, 891.

Argument was heard in the 1952 Term, and reargument was heard this Term on certain questions propounded by the Court.[3]

Reargument was largely devoted to the circumstances surrounding the adoption of the Fourteenth Amendment in 1868. It covered exhaustively consideration of the Amendment in Congress, ratification by the states, then existing practices in racial segregation, and the views of proponents and opponents of the Amendment. This discussion and our own investigation convince us that, although these sources cast some light, it is not enough to resolve the problem with which we are faced. At best, they are inconclusive. The most avid proponents of the post-War Amendments undoubtedly intended them to remove all legal distinctions among "all persons born or naturalized in the United States." Their opponents, just as certainly, were antagonistic to both the letter and the spirit of the Amendments and wished them to have the most limited effect. What others in Congress and the state legislatures had in mind cannot be determined with any degree of certainty.

An additional reason for the inconclusive nature of the Amendment's history, with respect to segregated schools, is the status of public education at that time.[4] In the South, the movement toward

[3] 345 U.S. 972. The Attorney General of the United States participated both Terms as *amicus curiae*.

[4] For a general study of the development of public education prior to the Amendment, see Butts and Cremin, *A History of Education in American Culture* (1953), Pts. I, II; Cubberley, Public Education in the United States (1934 ed.), cc. II-XII. School practices current at the time of the adoption of the Fourteenth Amendment are described in Butts and Cremin, *supra,* at 269-275; Cubberley, *supra,* at 288-339, 408-431; Knight, *Public Education in the South* (1922), cc. VIII, IX. See also H. Ex. Doc. No. 315, 41st Cong., 2d Sess. (1871). Although the demand for free public schools followed substantially the same pattern in both the North and the South, the development in the South did not begin to gain momentum until about 1850, some twenty years after that in the North. The reasons for the somewhat slower development in the South (*e.g.,* the rural character of the South and the different regional attitudes toward state assistance) are well explained in Cubberley, *supra,* at 408-423. In the country as a whole, but particularly in the South, the War virtually stopped all progress in public education. *Id.,* at 427-428. The low status of Negro education in all sections of the country, both before and immediately after the War, is described in Beale, *A History of Freedom of Teaching in American Schools* (1941), 112-132, 175-195. Compulsory school attendance laws were not generally adopted until after the ratification

free common schools, supported by general taxation, had not yet taken hold. Education of white children was largely in the hands of private groups. Education of Negroes was almost nonexistent, and practically all of the race were illiterate. In fact, any education of Negroes was forbidden by law in some states. Today, in contrast, many Negroes have achieved outstanding success in the arts and sciences as well as in the business and professional world. It is true that public school education at the time of the Amendment had advanced further in the North, but the effect of the Amendment on Northern States was generally ignored in the congressional debates. Even in the North, the conditions of public education did not approximate those existing today. The curriculum was usually rudimentary; ungraded schools were common in rural areas; the school term was but three months a year in many states; and compulsory school attendance was virtually unknown. As a consequence, it is not surprising that there should be so little in the history of the Fourteenth Amendment relating to its intended effect on public education.

In the first cases in this Court construing the Fourteenth Amendment, decided shortly after its adoption, the Court interpreted it as proscribing all state-imposed discriminations against the Negro race.[5] The doctrine of "separate but equal" did not make its ap-

---

of the Fourteenth Amendment, and it was not until 1918 that such laws were in force in all the states. Cubberley, *supra*, at 563-565.

[5] *Slaughter-House Cases*, 16 Wall. 36, 67-72 (1873); *Strauder* v. *West Virginia*, 100 U.S. 303, 307-308 (1880):

"It ordains that no State shall deprive any person of life, liberty, or property, without due process of law, or deny to any person within its jurisdiction the equal protection of the laws. What is this but declaring that the law in the States shall be the same for the black as for the white; that all persons, whether colored or white, shall stand equal before the laws of the States, and, in regard to the colored race, for whose protection the amendment was primarily designed, that no discrimination shall be made against them by law because of their color? The words of the amendment, it is true, are prohibitory, but they contain a necessary implication of a positive immunity, or right, most valuable to the colored race,—the right to exemption from unfriendly legislation against them distinctively as colored,—exemption from legal discriminations, implying inferiority in civil society, lessening the security of their enjoyment of the rights which others enjoy, and discriminations which are steps towards reducing them to the condition of a subject race."

See also *Virginia* v. *Rives*, 100 U.S. 313, 318 (1880); *Ex parte Virginia*, 100 U.S. 339, 344-345 (1880).

pearance in this Court until 1896 in the case of *Plessy* v. *Ferguson,* *supra,* involving not education but transportation.[6] American courts have since labored with the doctrine for over half a century. In this Court, there have been six cases involving the "separate but equal" doctrine in the field of public education.[7] In *Cumming* v. *County Board of Education,* 175 U.S. 528, and *Gong Lum* v. *Rice,* 275 U.S. 78, the validity of the doctrine itself was not challenged.[8] In more recent cases, all on the graduate school level, inequality was found in that specific benefits enjoyed by white students were denied to Negro students of the same educational qualifications. *Missouri ex rel. Gaines* v. *Canada,* 305 U.S. 337; *Sipuel* v. *Oklahoma,* 332 U.S. 631; *Sweatt* v. *Painter,* 339 U.S. 629; *McLaurin* v. *Oklahoma State Regents,* 339 U.S. 637. In none of these cases was it necessary to re-examine the doctrine to grant relief to the Negro plaintiff. And in *Sweatt* v. *Painter, supra,* the Court expressly reserved decision on the question whether *Plessy* v. *Ferguson* should be held inapplicable to public education.

In the instant cases, that question is directly presented. Here, unlike *Sweatt* v. *Painter,* there are findings below that the Negro and white schools involved have been equalized, or are being equalized, with respect to buildings, curricula, qualifications and salaries of teachers, and other "tangible" factors.[9] Our decision,

[6] The doctrine apparently originated in *Roberts* v. *City of Boston,* 59 Mass. 198, 206 (1850), upholding school segregation against attack as being violative of a state constitutional guarantee of equality. Segregation in Boston public schools was eliminated in 1855. Mass. Acts 1855, c. 256. But elsewhere in the North segregation in public education has persisted in some communities until recent years. It is apparent that such segregation has long been a nationwide problem, not merely one of sectional concern.

[7] See also *Berea College* v. *Kentucky,* 211 U.S. 45 (1908).

[8] In the *Cumming* case, Negro taxpayers sought an injunction requiring the defendant school board to discontinue the operation of a high school for white children until the board resumed operation of a high school for Negro children. Similarly, in the *Gong Lum* case, the plaintiff, a child of Chinese descent, contended only that state authorities had misapplied the doctrine by classifying him with Negro children and requiring him to attend a Negro school.

[9] In the Kansas case, the court below found substantial equality as to all such factors. 98 F. Supp. 797, 798. In the South Carolina case, the court below found that the defendants were proceeding "promptly and in good faith to comply with the court's decree." 103 F. Supp. 920, 921. In the Virginia case, the court below noted that the equalization program was already "afoot and progressing" (103 F. Supp. 337, 341); since then, we have been advised, in

therefore, cannot turn on merely a comparison of these tangible factors in the Negro and white schools involved in each of the cases. We must look instead to the effect of segregation itself on public education.

In approaching this problem, we cannot turn the clock back to 1868 when the Amendment was adopted, or even to 1896 when *Plessy* v. *Ferguson* was written. We must consider public education in the light of its full development and its present place in American life throughout the Nation. Only in this way can it be determined if segregation in public schools deprives these plaintiffs of the equal protection of the laws.

Today, education is perhaps the most important function of state and local governments. Compulsory school attendance laws and the great expenditures for education both demonstrate our recognition of the importance of education to our democratic society. It is required in the performance of our most basic public responsibilities, even service in the armed forces. It is the very foundation of good citizenship. Today it is a principal instrument in awakening the child to cultural values, in preparing him for later professional training, and in helping him to adjust normally to his environment. In these days, it is doubtful that any child may reasonably be expected to succeed in life if he is denied the opportunity of an education. Such an opportunity, where the state has undertaken to provide it, is a right which must be made available to all on equal terms.

We come then to the question presented: Does segregation of children in public schools solely on the basis of race, even though the physical facilities and other "tangible" factors may be equal, deprive the children of the minority group of equal educational opportunities? We believe that it does.

In *Sweatt* v. *Painter, supra,* in finding that a segregated law school for Negroes could not provide them equal educational opportunities, this Court relied in large part on "those qualities which are incapable of objective measurement but which make for greatness in a law school." In *McLaurin* v. *Oklahoma State Regents,*

---

the Virginia Attorney General's brief on reargument, that the program has now been completed. In the Delaware case, the court below similarly noted that the state's equalization program was well under way. 91 A. 2d 137, 149.

supra, the Court, in requiring that a Negro admitted to a white graduate school be treated like all other students, again resorted to intangible considerations: ". . . his ability to study, to engage in discussions and exchange views with other students, and, in general, to learn his profession." Such considerations apply with added force to children in grade and high schools. To separate them from others of similar age and qualifications solely because of their race generates a feeling of inferiority as to their status in the community that may affect their hearts and minds in a way unlikely ever to be undone. The effect of this separation on their educational opportunities was well stated by a finding in the Kansas case by a court which nevertheless felt compelled to rule against the Negro plaintiffs:

> Segregation of white and colored children in public schools has a detrimental effect upon the colored children. The impact is greater when it has the sanction of the law; for the policy of separating the races is usually interpreted as denoting the inferiority of the negro group. A sense of inferiority affects the motivation of a child to learn. Segregation with the sanction of law, therefore, has a tendency to [retard] the educational and mental development of negro children and to deprive them of some of the benefits they would receive in a racial[ly] integrated school system.[10]

Whatever may have been the extent of psychological knowledge at the time of *Plessy* v. *Ferguson,* this finding is amply supported by modern authority.[11] Any language in *Plessy* v. *Ferguson* contrary to this finding is rejected.

[10] A similar finding was made in the Delaware case: "I conclude from the testimony that in our Delaware society, State-imposed segregation in education itself results in the Negro children, as a class, receiving educational opportunities which are substantially inferior to those available to white children otherwise similarly situated." 87 A. 2d 862, 865.

[11] K. B. Clark, *Effect of Prejudice and Discrimination on Personality Development* (Midcentury White House Conference on Children and Youth, 1950); Witmer and Kotinsky, *Personality in the Making* (1952), c. VI; Deutscher and Chein, *The Psychological Effects of Enforced Segregation: A Survey of Social Science Opinion,* 26 J. Psychol. 259 (1948); Chein, *What Are the Psychological Effects of Segregation Under Conditions of Equal Facilities?,* 3 Int. J. Opinion and Attitude Res. 229 (1949); Brameld, *Educational Costs, in Discrimination and National Welfare* (MacIver, ed., 1949), 44-48; Frazier, *The Negro in the United States* (1949), 674-681. And see generally Myrdal, *An American Dilemma* (1944).

We conclude that in the field of public education the doctrine of "separate but equal" has no place. Separate educational facilities are inherently unequal. Therefore, we hold that the plaintiffs and others similarly situated for whom the actions have been brought are, by reason of the segregation complained of, deprived of the equal protection of the laws guaranteed by the Fourteenth Amendment. This disposition makes unnecessary any discussion whether such segregation also violates the Due Process Clause of the Fourteenth Amendment.[12]

Because these are class actions, because of the wide applicability of this decision, and because of the great variety of local conditions, the formulation of decrees in these cases presents problems of considerable complexity. On reargument, the consideration of appropriate relief was necessarily subordinated to the primary question—the constitutionality of segregation in public education. We have now announced that such segregation is a denial of the equal protection of the laws. In order that we may have the full assistance of the parties in formulating decrees, the cases will be restored to the docket, and the parties are requested to present further argument on Questions 4 and 5 previously propounded by the Court for the reargument this Term.[13] The Attorney General of the United States

[12] See *Bolling* v. *Sharpe, post,* p. 497, concerning the Due Process Clause of the Fifth Amendment.

[13] "4. Assuming it is decided that segregation in public schools violates the Fourteenth Amendment

"(a) would a decree necessarily follow providing that, within the limits set by normal geographic school districting, Negro children should forthwith be admitted to schools of their choice, or

"(b) may this Court, in the exercise of its equity powers, permit an effective gradual adjustment to be brought about from existing segregated systems to a system not based on color distinctions?

"5. On the assumption on which questions 4 (a) and (b) are based, and assuming further that this Court will exercise its equity powers to the end described in question 4 (b),

"(a) should this Court formulate detailed decrees in these cases;

"(b) if so, what specific issues should the decrees reach;

"(c) should this Court appoint a special master to hear evidence with a view to recommending specific terms for such decrees;

"(d) should this Court remand to the courts of first instance with directions to frame decrees in these cases, and if so what general directions should the decrees of this Court include and what procedures should the courts of first instance follow in arriving at the specific terms of more detailed decrees?"

is again invited to participate. The Attorneys General of the states requiring or permitting segregation in public education will also be permitted to appear as *amici curiae* upon request to do so by September 15, 1954, and submission of briefs by October 1, 1954.[14]

It is so ordered.

[14] See Rule 42, Revised Rules of this Court (effective July 1, 1954).

17 / RELIGION AS A SOURCE OF VALUES

Reinhold Niebuhr, one of the outstanding Protestant theologians and philosophers of our time, was born in Missouri in 1892, studied at a theological seminary in St. Louis, but received his Bachelor of Divinity from Yale in 1914. In 1916 he accepted a pastorate in Detroit, there becoming interested in the problems of an industrial society. Gradually he came to a position opposed both to the social gospel of liberal Protestantism and the privatism of orthodox Protestants, asserting that both misunderstood the nature and potentialities of man. He thus turned to the task of developing a theology suitable to the contemporary world.

In 1928 Niebuhr took a position on the faculty of Union Theological Seminary in New York City and there became the leading proponent of Protestant neo-orthodoxy, in which he emphasized his concept of original sin; that is, the recognition of the essentially sinful and tragic nature of man. Although Niebuhr has usually taken a liberal position on social and economic issues, he rejected the notion of the idea of the perfectibility of man and the idea of progress. He argued that all that man can hope to achieve is an unstable equilibrium between good and evil. Man's sin has been primarily his pride in his own power to control human destiny— his belief in his ability to achieve ultimate truths and social utopias.

SOURCE: Reinhold Niebuhr, "The Dilemma of Modern Man," *The Nation,* CLXIV, 8 (February 22, 1947), 205-9.

We are living in an age in which our social and historical imperatives may be fairly simply defined but not easily achieved. Our task is to create and re-create community within the terms set by a technical civilization. The constant elaboration of man's technical skills has created a potential world community, but this community cannot be actualized as easily as modern men had hoped. The same technical skills have created abundance in modern industrial communities; yet these communities all suffer from great social insecurity because they find it difficult to distribute the new wealth equitably enough to guarantee harmony and stability.

In such a historical situation the average person still interprets the faith by which he lives primarily in sociopolitical terms. He has faith in this or that social objective. Usually in the United States and in the Western world generally the objective is defined as "the democratic way of life." I do not believe that such a purely political objective constitutes an adequate "faith." It may define our primary moral obligation, or at least the social dimension of that obligation, but it does not define the meaning of our existence. Any adequate sense of the meaning of life must be able to comprehend not only what we ought to do but what we are. It must explain why we are creatures who do not find it easy, or even possible, to fulfil our highest obligation.

At the present moment the popular definition of our political ideal as the "democratic way of life" hides a very great dilemma, which is also a part of the total human situation. For the world is divided between different types of "democrats," between those who would sacrifice freedom, or have already sacrificed it, for the sake of an equalitarian and collectivist democracy and those who would make no sacrifice of any freedom in the interest of justice. In the international community this cleavage may result in a world conflict between two cohorts of world-savers holding contradictory views of democracy. In national communities it may still lead to the most tragic internecine conflicts. The truth obviously lies somewhere between these two creeds; but it is difficult to find, precisely because political creeds have been invested with a religious aura by a supposedly irreligious age. This whole development rather refutes John Dewey's hope, expressed some years ago in his "Common Faith," that men of good-will would agree on social and moral objectives, once modern culture had dissolved the irrelevant loyalties of historical religions. We have, as Americans, a particularly embarrassing position in this debate or conflict between contradictory conceptions of democracy. For America in general, and the American plutocracy in particular, has a more uncritical confidence in the organic relation between "free enterprise" and democracy than any other nation; and this type of bigotry may do more damage to the world community and the cause of justice than any religious bigotry ever did.

Even if this contradiction in the definition of our democratic objectives did not exist, it would still be impossible to define the meaning of human existence purely in terms of some social and political objective—partly because no human life can be completely contained within the bounds of the social and historical dimension of life, and partly because we do not either individually or collectively move as easily or surely toward ideal goals as past generations have assumed. Our age is secular, either non-Christian or anti-Christian, in the main outlines of its basic creed. It has disavowed the historical religious faiths partly because their symbols seem outmoded in an age of science but chiefly because modern men find the tragic view of life implicit in religion unacceptable and the old theories of redemption irrelevant. A message of redemption which offered men and nations life only through death and declared that men could be saved only through repentance seemed completely irrelevant to an age which saw history moving forward to ever more impressive elaborations of human power and freedom. There was nothing the matter with human life which historical growth could not cure.

The implicit faith of the past two centuries has hardly prepared us for the kind of frustration through which we must live in the next century or two. For we have been given the task of creating community in larger dimensions than any one or two centuries can accomplish. The frustrations of our age become pathetic rather than tragic when we have no means of either anticipating or comprehending the character of our present experiences. The one unifying element in all strands of modern culture was the idea of progress. We had faith in a redemptive history. This faith, which supposedly made all other interpretations of life completely incredible, is now progressively disclosing itself as the most incredible of all interpretations of life. This refutation of the culture of modern man by contemporary history may be regarded as the real spiritual crisis of our day.

When the atomic bomb fell upon Hiroshima it brought more than one chapter in both political and cultural history to a symbolic conclusion. It particularly concluded that chapter of Western spiritual history, beginning in the Renaissance, which regarded history as a kind of God and time as a kind of Christ. It was an age which assumed that technical progress, which continually increased man's power over nature and freedom from natural limitations, would inevitably contribute to human welfare and happiness. It was an age which assumed that man's increased mobility and the wider range of his eyes, ears, and voice, transfigured by microscope and telescope, telegraph and radio, would inevitably lead to the enlargement of the human community. Actually mechanical advances have only created a potential, and not an actual, world community, and have meanwhile destroyed many of the organic forms of community which gave life sanity and stability in older cultures.

We have had to learn that history is neither a God nor a redeemer. The real fact is that while history solves many problems, it aggravates rather than mitigates the basic incongruities of human existence. Man is a finite and contingent creature, with some sense of universal value transcending his own existence but unfortunately inclined to endow the contingent values of his life or culture, of his truth or loyalty, with an absolute significance which it does not deserve. He thereby finds community with his fellow-men as difficult as it is necessary; particularly since his fellow-men are engaged in the same idolatrous process. Man can neither live alone, not being self-sufficient, nor easily come to terms with his fellow-men. The same instruments which extend the range of possible community also extend the range of man's impulse to domination over his fellows. Thus history pitches the drama of life on continually higher levels, but the essentials of the drama remain the same.

The fact that history is endlessly creative but not redemptive might have been more apparent to modern man had it not been for another illusion in modern culture. This other illusion is closely related to the idea of progress and is indeed frequently the basis for it. It is the illusion that the so-called "methods of science" or "impartial scientific inquiry" or "scientific objectivity" are actually the instruments by which mankind rises to higher and higher degrees of perfection. There are forms of the idea of progress which trust primarily in the extension of the evolutionary process of biology into the realm of history. But more frequently historical progress is assumed to depend upon the ability of man gradually to rise from his position as a creature of natural and historical forces to become their master. The instrument by which this is to be accomplished is science. By scientific impartiality man presumably rises from finite to universal perspectives, from interested to disinterested appraisal of problems of justice, from prejudice and passion to godlike serenity and impartiality. Science will not only unlock the mysteries of existence which have remained closed to the poetic and religious imagination and to the speculations of philosophy but will redeem man from the fragmentary and partial character of his life and actions and guarantee action of universal validity.

Sometimes it is assumed that the methods of science will make men moral merely by making them rational. Sometimes it is believed that science should be used to control the dark and irrational forces in human nature, "that the same science which has altered the face of nature can change the habits of men." Sometimes the continued egotism and irrationality of individuals are assumed, but it is believed that a "scientific" politics will be able to manage social forces as readily as man now manages the forces of nature. The end product of these illusions is the type of rationalism which dreams of setting up a world government containing scientifically tested constitutional instruments for equilibrating all the vitalities of a community of nations and for arbitrating or, if necessary, suppressing every political conflict.

A simple fact has been obscured by this cult of redemption through science. Man is a creature whose rational and vital processes are in organic unity, and there is no "scientific method" by which he can escape from the hopes, fears, ambitions, and anxieties of his own individual existence or those of his nation, civilization, or ethnic group. In all problems pertaining to the security or the meaning of his own life or the justice of his conflict with some competing life or vitality, he is never the disinterested observer but an interested participant. In so far as impartiality is possible, it is a moral and religious as much as a scientific achievement. A contrite recognition of the interested character of our views and actions must always lie behind the achievement of relative disinterestedness.

The achievement involves the whole of the personality and is therefore not purely intellectual or scientific.

Modern culture has wittingly or unwittingly followed the thought of Comte, who believed that the history of the world could be divided into three ages—the theological, the metaphysical, and the scientific—and who saw the possibility of solving all human problems in the third and final stage of human development by the application of the scientific method to man's social existence. Actually the ability of science to achieve impartial and universally valid judgments rests partly upon the sharply circumscribed fields of inquiry in which science looks for causal relations and partly upon the fact that a natural science, which investigates the determined sequences of nature, is under no temptation to weigh evidence or make hazardous judgments on such imponderables as human motives.

But the wider the field of inquiry becomes, the more plainly will even the natural sciences betray themselves to be under the guidance of presuppositions, implicit or explicit metaphysical assumptions, which are not the consequence but the basis of the inquiry. If it is historical rather than biological or geological sequence which is under inquiry, there is no strictly "scientific" method of judging the motives which prompt human actions or of comparing competing vitalities in history. Every judgment of fact is also a value judgment, presupposing a norm. The norm is itself historically conditioned, and the application of the norm to the stuff of history is twice conditioned.

This fact does not invalidate the social and historical sciences or prove that they ought to be reduced to statistical proportions in order to become purer sciences. Both the logical and the analytical powers of reason remain instruments by which partial and particular points of view are corrected, and the whole stuff of historical reality is brought under examination. We must continue to seek to understand what things are and how they came to be what they are in history as well as in nature. But there is no magic in either logic or the scientific method which will coerce men or nations to subordinate the particular to the universal interest or to correct the partial by a more universal insight. Reason in history remains permanently ambiguous, being both the servant and the master of all of history's vitalities.

There is, for instance, no "scientific method" which could guarantee that statesmen who must deal with the social and political consequences of atomic energy could arrive at the kind of "universal mind" which operated in the discovery of atomic energy. Statesmen who deal with this problem will betray "British," "American," or "Russian" bias, not because they are less intelligent than the scientists but because they are forced to approach the issue in terms of their responsibility to their respective nations. Their formulation of a solution is intimately and organically related to the hopes, fears, and ambitions of nations. They must deal with history as a vital and not a rational process. As a vital process it is always something less and something more than reason. It is less than rational in so far as the power impulses of nations express themselves as inexorably as the force of a stampeding herd of cattle. It is something more than rational in so far as human beings have aspirations and loyalties transcending both impulse and prudence. Man is a heaven-storming creature whose highest ideals are curiously compounded with his immediate and mundane interests. The Marxist dream of a universal classless society, mixed with the power impulses of a Russian state and the anxieties of a precarious dictatorship, is a nice symbol of what historical reality is like. Our so-called democratic world is a little more rational; but the mixture of democratic idealism and the quest for profits of a vast American economic machine must be almost as bewildering to the outside observer as the Russian mixture.

The collective mixtures of ideals and interests are more vivid than individual expressions of human spirituality, but every individual life is governed less by prudence and rationality and more by what lies below the level of reason and rises above the level of rational calculation than a scientific culture understands. One may be grateful for the fact that poets and novelists continued to bear testimony to these dimensions of life even in a scientific age, if they dealt at all authentically with the human scene. Because man in his grandeur and in his misery, in his high aspirations and in their egoistic corruption, is and always will be a more complex creature than modern culture has understood, his history is more tragic and his redemption from self-seeking, whether individual or collective, more difficult and always less final than we have assumed.

Old cultures and civilizations, reigning oligarchies and traditional social systems and structures do not quietly yield to the logic of a new historical development. They refuse to die in bed. They take the field, ostensibly to defend their "ideals" against some new barbarism, but also to preserve established interests against new vitalities. That is why we must march through any number of world wars before we can achieve world community; and why the world community which is within the grasp of human powers will be less stable and secure than our calculating world planners can realize. History presents us with constantly enlarged responsibilities. We must meet these responsibilities if we would remain human. The Nazis have shown us the perverse consequences of any effort to turn the clock back and "return to the womb" of tribal primitivism. We must move on. But there are neither securities nor fulfilments in history in which the heart can rest.

Since we are free spirits who transcend the historical process, as well as creatures who are involved in it, we crave for some ultimate security and fulfilment. But since history remains as fragmentary and as full of contradictions as our individual life-adventures, we can have such security and fulfilment only in an ultimate sense and only by faith. The kind of faith which adequately completes the temple of meaning will also reveal that our own egotism, and that of our nation, and not merely the egotism of competitor or foe is responsible for the tragic aspects of history. Thus contrition and faith go hand in hand.

In Christian piety the devout soul always beholds itself in a double relation to Christ. The perfect love, of which the Cross is the symbol, is regarded as the final norm of human goodness and defines what man ought to be. But man also knows himself to be the crucifier of the Christ. This expresses our understanding of the fact that life can only be brought to completion by a love in which the self is not concerned for itself but only for its fellows. But we also know that as individuals and as groups we seek our own. The justice we have achieved in history is a compromise between these two impulses; and the compromise is not achieved simply by calculation and prudence. Such pity and mercy as are insinuated into the cruelties and inhumanities of human life are the fruits of the contrition, which recognizes that the egotism we abhor in others is in us also. Fanaticism is always the product of self-righteousness.

Religion has produced as much fanaticism as contrition, because religion is never a good force per se, but merely the final conflict between human self-esteem and divine mercy. And the one is as frequently victorious as the other. A secular age imagined that it could exorcise fanaticism by disavowing religion. But an age which prides itself upon its scientific objectivity has actually sunk to new levels of cruelty, for the man who knows himself to be absolutely right through the benefit of science is as cruel as those who achieved this fanaticism by religious revelation. Not only Marxist fanatics are involved in the cruelties of our age, but democratic idealists also. The ancients were certainly not more merciless to their foes than we; no one has been so merciless to a vanquished foe as we since the Assyrians. We are pitiless because we do not know ourselves to be pitiable.

A secular age thought it would be sufficient to disavow the otherworldliness of religion in order to achieve a consistent and humane sense of responsibility for the commonweal. But the disavowal of an incredible heaven led to the avowal of incredible utopias; incredible because they defined an unconditioned good amid the conditions of nature [and] history. This persistent utopianism has generated fanatical furies of our day, for if the heaven of a classless society could be established on earth, would it be worth the price which the Communists are ready to pay? It is also responsible for the alternate fits of illusion and disillusion which distract us from our historic responsibilities.

Life is never completed, either individually or collectively; and it is never completely freed from chaos or from contradiction to its essential meaning. An adequate faith must understand this quality of life; but that is impossible without an explicit or implicit belief that a divine mercy can complete what we cannot complete. Such a faith may of course be corrupted and may beguile men from their pressing responsibilities; but the alternative secular idealism also leads to deep corruptions. It tempts men to seek in others, and never in themselves, the root of human misery. And if they finally find it in themselves, their optimism gives way to despair. The mood of this century compared with the optimism of the nineteenth century looks very much like the despair which all false optimism generates. . . .

18 / SCIENCE AS A SOURCE OF VALUES

B. F. Skinner, one of the most vocal leaders of the modern behavioral school of psychologists, was born in 1904 in Pennsylvania, graduated from Hamilton College in 1926, and took a Ph.D. from Harvard in 1931. He has been a member of the psychology department of Harvard University since 1948. Although his primary field of research has been in the control of human behavior, Skinner has ranged far from laboratory experiments to speculations on the implications for scientific control and manipulation of human beings. The most popular statement of his theories of behaviorism is Walden Two, *a novel published in 1948, in which he attempts to demonstrate how, by the use of modern psychological and behavioral techniques, a utopian community might be created. He has attempted to deal with the ethical questions of power, but maintains that the scientific method provides the only reliable means for the discovery of truth, even ethical truth.*

If we are not to rely solely upon accident for the innovations which give rise to cultural evolution, we must accept the fact that some kind of control of human behavior is inevitable. We cannot use good sense in human affairs unless someone engages in the design and construction of environmental conditions which affect the behavior of men. Environmental changes have always been the condition for the improvement of cultural patterns, and we can hardly use the more effective methods of science without making changes on a grander scale. We are all controlled by the world in which we live, and part of that world has been and will be constructed

SOURCE: B. F. Skinner, "Freedom and the Control of Men," *The American Scholar*, LVI (Winter, 1955-56), 56-59, 64-65.

by men. The question is this: Are we to be controlled by accident, by tyrants, or by ourselves in effective cultural design?

The danger of the misuse of power is possibly greater than ever. It is not allayed by disguising the facts. We cannot make wise decisions if we continue to pretend that human behavior is not controlled, or if we refuse to engage in control when valuable results might be forthcoming. Such measures weaken only ourselves, leaving the strength of science to others. The first step in a defense against tyranny is the fullest possible exposure of controlling techniques. A second step has already been taken successfully in restricting the use of physical force. Slowly, and as yet imperfectly, we have worked out an ethical and governmental design in which the strong man is not allowed to use the power deriving from his strength to control his fellow men. He is restrained by a superior force created for that purpose—the ethical pressure of the group, or more explicit religious and governmental measures. We tend to distrust superior forces, as we currently hesitate to relinquish sovereignty in order to set up an international police force. But it is only through such counter-control that we have achieved what we call peace—a condition in which men are not permitted to control each other through force. In other words, control itself must be controlled.

Science has turned up dangerous processes and materials before. To use the facts and techniques of a science of man to the fullest extent without making some monstrous mistake will be difficult and obviously perilous. It is no time for self-deception, emotional indulgence, or the assumption of attitudes which are no longer useful. Man is facing a difficult test. He must keep his head now, or he must start again—a long way back.

Those who reject the scientific conception of man must, to be logical, oppose the methods of science as well. The position is often supported by predicting a series of dire consequences which are to follow if science is not checked. A recent book by Joseph Wood Krutch, *The Measure of Man,* is in this vein. Mr. Krutch sees in the growing science of man the threat of an unexampled tyranny over men's minds. If science is permitted to have its way, he insists, "we may never be able really to think again." A controlled culture will, for example, lack some virtue inherent in disorder. We have emerged from chaos through a series of happy accidents, but in an engineered culture it will be "impossible for the unplanned to erupt again." But there is no virtue in the accidental character of an accident, and the diversity which arises from disorder can not only be duplicated by design but vastly extended. The experimental method is superior to simple observation just because it multiplies "accidents" in a systematic coverage of the possibilities. Technology offers many familiar examples. We no longer wait for immunity to disease to develop from a series of accidental exposures, nor do we wait for natural mutations in sheep and cotton to produce better fibers; but we continue to make use of such accidents when they occur, and we certainly do not prevent them. Many of the things we value have emerged from the clash of ignorant armies on darkling plains, but it is not therefore wise to encourage ignorance and darkness.

It is not always disorder itself which we are told we shall miss but certain admirable qualities in men which flourish only in the presence of disorder. A man rises above an unpropitious childhood to a position of eminence, and since we cannot give a plausible account of the action of so complex an environment, we attribute the achievement to some admirable faculty in the man himself. But such "faculties" are suspiciously like the explanatory fictions against which the history of science warns us. We admire Lincoln for rising above a deficient school system, but it was not necessarily something *in him* which permitted him to become an educated man in spite of it. His educational environment was certainly unplanned, but it could nevertheless have made a full contribution to his mature behavior. He was a rare man, but the circumstances of his childhood were rare too. We do not give Franklin Delano Roosevelt the same credit for becoming an educated man with the help of Groton and Harvard, although the same behavioral processes may have been involved. The founding of Groton and Harvard somewhat reduced the possibility that fortuitous combinations of circumstances would erupt to produce other Lincolns. Yet the founders can hardly be condemned for attacking an admirable human quality.

Another predicted consequence of a science of man is an excessive uniformity. We are told that effective control—whether governmental, religious, educational, economic or social—will produce a race of men who differ from each other only through relatively refractory genetic differences. That would probably be bad design, but we must admit that we are not now pursuing another course from choice. In a modern school, for example, there is usually a syllabus which specifies what every student is to learn by the end of each year. This would be flagrant regimentation if anyone expected every student to comply. But some will be poor in particular subjects, others will not study, others will not remember what they have been taught, and diversity is assured. Suppose, however, that we someday possess such effective educational techniques that every student will in fact be put in possession of all the behavior specified in a syllabus. At the end of the year, all students will correctly answer all questions on the final examination and "must all have prizes." Should we reject such a system on the grounds that in making all students excellent it has made them all alike? Advocates of the theory of a special faculty might contend that an important advantage of the present system is that the good student learns *in spite of* a system which is so defective that it is currently producing bad students as well. But if really effective techniques are available, we cannot avoid the problem of design simply by preferring the status quo. At what point should education be deliberately inefficient?

Such predictions of the havoc to be wreaked by the application of science to human affairs are usually made with surprising confidence. They not only show a faith in the orderliness of human behavior; they presuppose an established body of knowledge with the help of which it can be positively asserted that the changes which scientists propose to make will have quite specific results— albeit not the results they foresee. But the predictions made by the critics of science must be held to be equally fallible and subject also to empirical test. . . .

Far from being a threat to the tradition of Western democracy, the growth of a science of man is a consistent and probably inevitable part of it. In turning to the external conditions which shape and maintain the behavior of men, while questioning the reality of inner qualities and faculties to which human achievements were once attributed, we turn from the ill-defined and remote to the observable and manipulable. Though it is a painful step, it has far-reaching consequences, for it not only sets higher standards of human welfare but shows us how to meet them. A change in a theory of human nature cannot change the facts. The achievements of man in science, art, literature, music and morals will survive any interpretation we place upon them. The uniqueness of the individual is unchallenged in the scientific view. Man, in short, will remain man. (There will be much to admire for those who are so inclined. Possibly the noblest achievement to which man can aspire, even according to present standards, is to accept himself for what he is, as that is revealed to him by the methods which he devised and tested on a part of the world in which he had only a small personal stake.)

If Western democracy does not lose sight of the aims of humanitarian action, it will welcome the almost fabulous support of its own science of man and will strengthen itself and play an important role in building a better world for everyone. But if it cannot put its "democratic philosophy" into proper historical perspective—if, under the control of attitudes and emotions which it generated for other purposes, it now rejects the help of science—then it must be prepared for defeat. For if we continue to insist that science has nothing to offer but a new and more horrible form of tyranny, we may produce just such a result by allowing the strength of science to fall into the hands of despots. And if, with luck, it were to fall instead to men of good will in other political communities, it would be perhaps a more ignominious defeat; for we should then, through a miscarriage of democratic principles, be forced to leave to others the next step in man's long struggle to control nature and himself.